BE
THE **BBQ**
PITMASTER

BE
THE BBQ
PITMASTER

A REGIONAL SMOKER COOKBOOK
CELEBRATING AMERICA'S BEST BARBECUE

WILL BUDIAMAN

SONOMA
PRESS

THIS BOOK IS DEDICATED TO ANYONE
WHO PRACTICES THEIR CRAFT
WITH INTEGRITY AND RESPECT.

CONTENTS

INTRODUCTION

What an exciting time it is to live and eat in America! We have more choices than ever about what to eat, as well as when, how, and where to eat it. You can have an amazing meal in a parking lot—when pork is carved off a sizzling spit for tacos al pastor, who cares where the truck is parked? Delight in hand-pulled noodles from your favorite takeout joint, delivered with a few taps on your phone. Or you can go all out at, say, a three-Michelin-star restaurant, and have exquisite hamachi crudo. We really are spoiled for choice.

And this is a good problem to have. We've come to expect and crave variety when it's time for the next meal, which is why many Americans have such a hard time answering the simple question: What is American food?

Here then, is a simple answer: barbecue.

Lest we forget, we have our very own food tradition that deserves to be recognized and celebrated. Barbecue is a pillar of American cookery. It originated from our nation's early roots and even played an important role throughout its political history.

Barbecue, like most of the world's great cuisines, has regional variations. And you can bet that wherever there's a strong barbecue tradition, people are fiercely proud of it. For someone from Piedmont, North Carolina, barbecue is pork shoulder chopped up and served with a vinegary sauce. In central Texas, it's beef brisket. Kansas City? Burnt ends. Kentucky? Mutton. (Yes, served with black barbecue sauce.) For each of these folks, there is only one way to do barbecue: their way.

But cook your way through the recipes here, and you'll see they're all equally worth celebrating.

This book will guide you every step of the way, with in-depth information on ingredients, equipment, and technique. You'll learn about the different regions with expert advice from pitmasters, and recipes that recreate traditional meals. For those who like a challenge, we've arranged the smoking recipes according to difficulty, allowing you to build your skill set.

All barbecue—no matter where it's from—is meat cooked low and slow, flavored with smoke from smoldering wood. You can change the meat, you can change the sides, you can change the sauce. (Heck, you can even throw out the sauce.) But no matter where it's from, there are three ingredients you can't change: Meat. Smoke. And, most importantly, time. So, if you're into slow food, this is about as slow as it gets. And that is definitely a good thing.

ONE

AN OVERVIEW OF BARBECUE FUNDAMENTALS

BBQ BASICS

Growing up, I always got a thrill from sinking my teeth into some saucy baby back ribs, and the messier, the better. For a kid, it was a chance to let loose because for once it was okay—no, encouraged—to make a huge mess at the table. No utensils needed; just the implements we were born with. To this day, a rack of wet ribs is still one of my favorite foods, even though I may not put my whole face into it like I used to.

Making barbecue shares the same appeal. It's a chance to let loose, unplug from the information overload that's part of everyday life, and sit a spell. When barbecuing, it's just you and a big, beautiful piece of meat. And while it isn't something that demands your absolute attention every single minute, you can't exactly get up and leave, either. So, you think about things, maybe invite a friend over, and drink some beer. And that's a precious thing, indeed.

A VERY BRIEF SURVEY OF AMERICAN BARBECUE

Before the first European settlers arrived, Native Americans had long been barbecuing meat, according to food historian Robert F. Moss. Along the East Coast and in the Caribbean, it was common practice to cook whole animals by placing them on wooden racks elevated over the dying embers of a fire, just high enough to make sure they cooked low and slow, absorbing the flavor of the smoke. Modern-day pitmasters would recognize this technique because it really hasn't changed much.

When Jamestown, Virginia, was founded in 1607, colonists brought pigs with them that multiplied quickly in the surrounding forests. The residents loved to entertain, and cooking whole pigs the Native American way quickly became the centerpiece of social and political gatherings.

As settlers branched out into the Carolinas, they brought this barbecue tradition with them. Although pork remained the meat of choice there, as settlements spread farther south into Georgia and Alabama and westward into Tennessee, Kentucky, and Texas, practicality trumped tradition; settlers became less particular about what they barbecued. A nineteenth-century barbecue could involve anything from chicken and mutton to oxen and squirrel.

It wasn't until the early twentieth century that barbecue began to take on today's regional characteristics. With the construction of highways and more people moving into cities, demand for barbecue boomed, and the famed "barbecue men" of the era, who were local hobbyists, opened restaurants. The four most popular styles during this time—Texas, Carolina, Kansas City, and Memphis—can be traced back to three factors.

One was a lack of refrigeration. Since meat couldn't be transported long distances, using local ingredients made sense. In the plains of Texas, cattle were easy to raise; in Carolina, hogs were plentiful.

Another was migration and culture. African Americans were crucial to the development of barbecue throughout its history, but were particularly influential in Kansas City and Memphis. After the Civil War, many African Americans came to these cities from the Deep South in search of better opportunities. They brought their recipes with them and opened restaurants in their new homes. In many places, traditions brought to this country by Greek, German, and Czech immigrants also played a major role.

Lastly, pitmasters passed down their knowledge to the next generation through apprenticeship. This guaranteed that regional styles would remain in place as time passed.

What defined barbecue nearly led to its downfall, however. The 1950s saw the birth of fast food restaurants and, according to Moss, their success was based on "speed, standardization, and low labor costs." Barbecue was the opposite of all these things. Chains that attempted to merge the two concepts either failed or shifted to less labor-intensive items such as burgers and fries.

Today, Americans are enjoying a renewed interest in barbecue, and fast food isn't quite as popular as it used to be. Competitive circuits across the country have generated an awareness of barbecue as a regional food, helping preserve tradition, while immigrant influences continue its evolution. Thanks to these driving forces, the future of barbecue looks promising once again.

REGIONAL STYLES AND DIFFERENCES

What exactly defines a regional style of barbecue? Three things: the types of proteins smoked, the way they are served, and the sauces (if any) and sides that accompany them. Here is a brief overview of the different regions that will be covered in greater detail in part two.

Carolinas. Roughly speaking, the Carolinas itself can be divided into three regions: Eastern North Carolina, the Piedmont area of North Carolina, and South Carolina. In Eastern North Carolina, barbecue is the whole hog flavored with hickory or oak, chopped and served with a thin vinegar and red pepper sauce. Accompaniments include North Carolina Brunswick Stew (page 85), Hushpuppies (page 83), and Slaw with Mayonnaise Dressing (page 86). In contrast, in the western part of the state, or the Piedmont, restaurants serve chopped pork shoulder with a tomato-vinegar sauce. Sides are similar, except for Barbecue Slaw (page 88). In South Carolina, the famous joints are pretty evenly divided between serving the whole animal or just the shoulder, but what really sets them apart is the tangy Mustard Barbecue Sauce (page 98). Contrary to popular belief, though, it's not served everywhere in the state. South Carolina's sauce boundaries echo the North's near the border, while mustard is served in the central part, and a bit of ketchup appears on the scene to the west near Georgia. As for sides, you can't have South Carolina barbecue without Pulled Pork Hash (page 91). Tyson Ho, owner of Arrogant Swine, trained under the legendary Ed Mitchell, and he's got plenty to say about Carolina barbecue in chapter 4.

Texas. Texas is a big state, so it's no surprise that when it comes to barbecue, most folks argue that it's divided into at least four regions. In East Texas, things aren't terribly different from what you'll find in neighboring Mississippi and Alabama; hickory-smoked pork shoulder and ribs reign supreme. They're served with sweet and spicy tomato-based sauce and some Baked Pinto Beans (page 176) and slaw. In Central Texas, it's all about brisket, sausage, and pork ribs smoked with oak or pecan. Popular sides are similar, although you're more likely to find German Potato Salad (page 187). In West Texas, the order of the day is "cowboy style," or beef cooked with mesquite, which is plentiful in that area and a good match for the flavor of beef. Lastly, in the barbacoa region near the Mexican border, the tradition of cooking whole cow heads in the ground persists. William Weisiger, head pitmaster at Dallas's Ten 50 BBQ, and John Tesar, executive chef of the well-regarded restaurants Knife and Oak, both also in Dallas, offer their insights in chapter 7.

Memphis. Memphians love pork, and their pulled pork sandwiches are a must-try thanks to a tomato-based sauce that has a depth of flavor that can only come from molasses. The city's other claim to fame is dry-rubbed pork ribs, which by all rights don't need any sauce. Sides, too, are interesting, all of them involving (what else?) barbecue: Barbecue Spaghetti (page 152), Barbecue Pizza (page 154), and Barbecue Nachos (page 151). Clint Cantwell, Memphis resident and editor of Grillocracy.com, knows just about everyone who's anyone in the world of Memphis barbecue, and he shares his stories in chapter 6.

Kansas City. When it comes to meat, Kansas City is a bit of a hodgepodge. There, you'll find restaurants serving ribs, pulled pork, chicken, ham, and even turkey. And then, of course, there are the infamous "burnt ends," what some might call the best part of a brisket. They come from the point, the smaller part of the brisket that develops a high bark-to-meat ratio as it cooks. Wood choice varies among hickory, oak, or pecan, and if you've ever bought sauce from the supermarket, you're familiar with the Kansas City style. Sides include the usual suspects of Kansas City–Style Baked Beans (page 120), slaw, and French Fries (page 124). Michael Ollier, executive chef for Certified Angus Beef, talks about the city's claim to fame—burnt ends—in chapter 8.

Alabama and Mississippi. It's not just about "Sweet Home Alabama" Barbecue Sauce (page 218) in Alabama, but if that's what you're after, you'll find plenty of it in the northern part of the state, where it's the perfect accompaniment to Beer Can Chicken (page 201). Pork ribs and shoulder smoked over hickory or pecan and served with a spicy, tomato-based sauce are famous here. Cool your palate with bites of Mustard Slaw (page 213). David and Joe Maluff, owners of Full Moon Bar-B-Que in Birmingham, share some recipes in chapter 8.

Kentucky. Mutton was common in the early days of barbecue, but now the tradition is confined to the western reaches of Kentucky. There, it's served with Black Barbecue Sauce (page 224) made with Worcestershire.

Georgia. Chopped pork flavored with oak and hickory is often served without sauce, but if there is sauce, it's made with ketchup and molasses. The iconic side dish is Georgia-Style Brunswick Stew (page 215), made with a variety of meats. Ryan Lamon, a second-generation Georgia pitmaster, highlights the ins and outs of the Georgia style in chapter 8.

THE PROCESS OF SMOKING MEAT

Heat, moisture, and smoke: These are the three elements needed to transform any cut of meat into barbecue. This section discusses each of these in turn; by the end, you should have a better understanding of how they work together.

When pitmasters talk about barbecue, they often talk about cooking "low and slow." What, exactly, does this mean, and why is it important?

Depending on who you talk to, the ideal temperature for barbecuing lies somewhere in the range of 225°F and 275°F. Any higher than that and you're getting into grilling territory; any lower than that and you end up preserving the meat rather than cooking it.

Traditional barbecue mostly deals with tough cuts of meat that have lots of connective tissue, or collagen. Pork shoulder, beef brisket, and ribs are good examples. Given time, heat breaks this collagen down into gelatin, which melts into the meat and gives it that lip-smacking mouthfeel people associate with good barbecue. It may be tempting to crank the heat and speed up this process, but collagen is a fickle thing: Try to hurry it along too much, and it wrings all the water out of the meat like a wet rag, and you end up with really dry barbecue.

That's because moisture is important, too. We're talking about the moisture on the surface of the meat and the ambient humidity inside the cooking chamber. Applying a dry rub to the meat at least 1 hour before cooking and letting it come to room temperature will draw out moisture from the interior to the surface. The dry rub should always contain salt, as this is the ingredient that does all the heavy lifting. To create and maintain ambient humidity, which will maintain moisture on the surface of the meat, keep a full water pan inside the cooker at all times. Moisture is key to helping smoke stick to the surface of the meat and penetrate to the interior. In addition, the interaction between heat, moisture, and smoke on the surface helps create a nice crust, or bark, through a series of chemical processes known as the Maillard reaction. While the browning of foods is the best-known result of the Maillard reaction, it's also responsible for the flavors and aromas of the food that come about from the rearranging of amino acids and certain simple sugars.

Lastly, without smoke, barbecue wouldn't be barbecue. No matter what type of fuel you're using to generate heat—charcoal, gas, or electricity—you'll also need wood to generate smoke. (Of course, if wood is your fuel, then you're all set.) Depending on your smoker, you'll need wood chips, chunks, or logs. Any type of hardwood can be used as long as it's non-resinous; resinous woods produce bitter-tasting smoke. Most people just use whatever is readily available, but if you're a stickler for authenticity, the recipes in part two have information on the woods typically used for each region's barbecue.

NOW THAT'S A PARTY

To commemorate his triumph in the 1922 Oklahoma gubernatorial race, John C. "Jack" Walton held a public barbecue and invited the entire state. Farmers gave away thousands of animals for the event— including the usual cows, pigs, and sheep—but also some questionable critters such as opossums, reindeer, and even a bear. About 500 people were involved in cooking, and a crowd of at least 100,000 descended on the feast, according to the *Dallas Morning News*.

One more thing: wrapping. At some point, the meat you're smoking will reach its saturation point. A deeply colored crust will have formed on the surface, and the meat won't absorb any more smoke. This is when some pitmasters wrap the meat in aluminum foil or butcher paper to continue cooking the inside of it without losing any more moisture. Others say this is completely unnecessary and only adds another step to the process. In some circles, wrapping is a controversial practice; in part two, you'll hear from pitmasters on both sides of the issue. Whether you choose to do it is up to you.

A PRIMER ON COOKERS

Charcoal or gas? Wood or electric? Here, you'll find detailed information on the types of smokers available on the market today, as well as basic information on how to get started using them.

▶ CHARCOAL SMOKERS

When it comes to charcoal smokers, you've got two choices: offset models and vertical water smokers. The terms refer to the location of the firebox in relation to the cooking compartment. Simply put, the firebox is the chamber where the charcoal and wood go, and the cooking compartment is where the meat goes.

In offset smokers, the firebox is located to one side of the cooking compartment. In most models, the cooking compartment is similar to a large barrel, cut in half horizontally to create a hinged opening. Vents along the side draw in smoke from the firebox and allow you to adjust the temperature in the cooking compartment. Opening the vents allows more oxygen inside, stokes the fire, and increases the temperature; closing them reduces the temperature. At the opposite end of the cooking chamber, a chimney lets smoke escape and promotes circulation. To maintain ample humidity inside the cooking chamber, it is highly recommended that you place a water pan directly on the grates.

Vertical water smokers come with a water pan built in, and they are an inexpensive way to start your barbecuing experience. For *Star Wars* fans out there, most models look a bit like R2-D2. The bubble-shaped lid on top encloses the cooking chamber, which has one or two grates; just below is the water pan, followed by the firebox. Like offset models, good vertical water smokers should also have adjustable vents. The location of the water pan allows it to also function as a drip pan, capturing any melting fat from the meat as it cooks. This keeps it from dripping down onto the fire and causing flare-ups.

If you're using a charcoal smoker, it's most important to know how to start your fire safely. It is strongly recommended that you use a chimney starter, which allows you to light the charcoal before putting it in the firebox. To use one, follow these simple steps:

1 Stuff the bottom of the chimney starter with newspaper or any clean scrap paper you have on hand. Don't pack it down too tight.

2 Place the charcoal on top. Most chimneys will accept about a gallon of charcoal, but don't overdo it; leave some room near the top so that you can easily transfer the lit charcoal to the firebox.

3 Light the paper and wait for the charcoal to light. If it fails to light, add more paper to the bottom and light it again. You may need to do this a few times before the charcoal lights.

4 Wait until all the charcoal is burning, put on some gloves, and dump the lit charcoal into the firebox. Add wood that has been soaked for at least 30 minutes to the charcoal, to create smoke.

5 Set the chimney starter aside to cool.

6 To keep a steady temperature going in the cooking chamber, you'll need to repeat this process, adding charcoal and wood periodically. How often you'll need to do so depends on the quality of the insulation in your cooking chamber and the weather conditions (temperature, humidity, and wind), but give yourself ample time to complete this process; start about 15 or 20 minutes before you'll actually need to add the lit charcoal to the firebox.

▶ ELECTRIC SMOKERS

If you're looking for the ultimate in convenience, you may want to consider an electric smoker. Purists may complain that using one robs barbecue of its soul, but it's hard to argue with the consistent results. Electric smokers have digitally controlled thermostats that allow you to set the temperature at the push of a button and virtually eliminate the need to worry about maintaining steady heat inside the cooking chamber. In this respect, it's a bit like using a slow cooker, though you probably shouldn't walk away from one for too long, and certainly don't leave the house.

The best electric smokers are mechanically fed pellet smokers. These are pricey, ranging from several hundred dollars on up to $4,000, but you definitely get what you pay for. They expose compressed hardwood pellets to a heating element at a steady rate in order to create smoke. Pellets come in the same varieties you would expect when purchasing wood—hickory, apple, mesquite, and so on—allowing you to customize the flavor of the smoke just as you can with any other smoker.

Since there are so many models of electric smokers out there, it's probably best to refer to your manufacturer's instructions for the specifics on how to get started, but here's a general overview that will apply to most models.

1 Find a suitable electrical outlet. Make sure that it is rated at the correct amperage for your cooker.

2 Plug in the cooker and turn it on. Set the desired temperature and allow the heating element to preheat to the temperature you want for your meats.

3 Add the pellets to the mechanical feeder and let the cooking chamber fill with smoke.

4 Place the meat inside the cooking chamber and add wood pellets periodically to maintain a steady supply of smoke.

▶ GAS SMOKERS

Gas smokers are nearly as convenient as electric smokers but without the hefty price tag—the cheapest ones start at $250. The typical design resembles a cabinet; inside, cooking racks sit above a water pan, which sits above another pan that holds the wood. At the base is the burner. Most gas smokers are powered by propane, so you'll just connect the unit to a standard 20-pound tank. Look for models that have two doors, one for the cooking chamber and another to access the wood.

Here are some basic steps to getting started but, as always, it's a good idea to read through your manual, too.

1 Connect the tank to the unit and open the valve. Light the burner; if it fails to light on the first try, turn off the valve, let the chamber air out, and start over.

2 Fill the water pan and wood pan.

3 Set the desired temperature and preheat.

4 Adjust the vents to maintain the desired temperature, and place the meat on the grates.

5 Add water and wood as necessary to maintain moisture and smoke.

▶ WOOD SMOKERS

If you're ready to take your barbecue to the next level, you may want to consider a wood smoker. In particular, if you're looking for the most pronounced smoke flavor, it's hard to beat a wood smoker since they use whole logs for fuel. They are well suited for advanced projects like smoking whole hogs but, as a result, tend to require a lot of real estate.

In terms of design, most have an offset firebox; some have a slight twist on the usual design in that the chimney is placed next to the firebox instead of at the opposite end, called a reverse flow smoker. In a reverse flow smoker, the smoke and heat run along a tunnel underneath the grates and make a U-turn at the end of the cooking chamber back toward the firebox, passing over the meat. Either design is fine; what matters most is the quality of construction.

Good wood smokers are pricey. While entry-level models start at a few hundred dollars, you'll generally want to avoid them. Manufacturers cut costs on low-end models by using thin metal, which makes it hard to maintain a steady temperature when cooking. Furthermore, thin metal is prone to rusting, reducing the life span of your equipment.

When shopping for a wood smoker, look for stainless steel that is at least ⅛ inch thick; thicker is always better. Make sure the doors have well-fitting seals and close tightly; the handles should be insulated. If you're shopping for a very large smoker, look for an insulated firebox as well. Last but not least, make sure the smoker has a drip pan or drain that will allow you to clean out the fat and juices that drip down through the grates as the meat cooks.

Once you've got your rig, it's time to start it up. Here are some guidelines to help you get going.

1 Have a good supply of wood on hand. It should not be freshly cut, ideally, but left out to dry for some time until it is no longer green. It should also be non-resinous. If necessary, cut some pieces down so that you have a variety of sizes.

2 Stack logs in the firebox in an interlocking pattern, leaving room in the first layer for kindling. Create kindling by coating some butcher paper with oil and wrapping some small pieces of wood with it. Place it into the gap, light it, and let the logs burn with the door open until there is a solid layer of glowing coals.

3 Add more wood to the coals with the firebox door still open. Wait until the smoke coming out of the chimney turns blue, then add the meat to the cooking chamber. Close the cooking chamber door, but leave the firebox door open during the entire cooking process.

4 Use different-size pieces of wood, as well as the vents, to control the temperature of the cooking chamber.

▶ SMOKER MAINTENANCE

A good smoker doesn't come cheap, so here are some tips on keeping it in top-notch condition.

Keep it seasoned. Regularly run your smoker at high temperature without anything in the cooking compartment, to burn off any accumulated deposits. An hour or so should be sufficient. If you have a charcoal or wood smoker, build the hottest fire you can; if you have a gas or electric smoker, set it to the highest temperature possible. Afterward, wipe down the interior and coat it all over with food-grade mineral oil or vegetable oil to protect against rust. If your smoker is brand new, you should perform this procedure before cooking anything for the first time, to burn off any undesirable substances left over from the manufacturing process.

Scrape away loose seasoning. As time passes, the layer of seasoning will erode. If you see any seasoning that is flaking off the cooking surfaces, scrape it off and reseason.

Protect against the elements. Especially in regions with inclement weather, a cover helps reduce wear and tear on your equipment when it's not in use.

Clean right away. Cleaning the grates immediately after you're finished cooking is a good habit to get into. If you wait until they cool, any ash or remaining food particles will stick to the grates and be more difficult to remove.

Keep it ready for the next smoke. After cleaning, dip a rag in vegetable oil and, using a pair of tongs, swab it over the grates so your smoker is ready to use next time.

Deep-clean once a year. Even with regular seasoning, over time, debris will accumulate in your cooker, which can result in flare-ups. Scrub the entire interior and use a paint scraper for more stubborn areas.

Remember to clean the chimney. If your smoker is equipped with a chimney, clean it out on a regular basis. Buildup will reduce airflow in the cooking chamber.

Be careful with the wires. If your smoker has any sensitive electronics, make sure not to get any cleaning solution or water on them.

Get rid of ash. Letting ash collect inside your smoker accelerates rusting. Use a shovel to remove it after each use; don't spray water inside the firebox.

Keep an eye out for rust. Even with regular ash removal, rust can still form inside your smoker, so it's a good idea to inspect for rust regularly. If you find some, scrape it off and repaint or reseason as necessary.

TO GRILL OR NOT TO GRILL

In everyday conversation, when most people say they're going to barbecue something, they're actually talking about grilling. Grilled burgers and hot dogs may be part of a typical backyard "barbecue," but it is not *barbecue* in the traditional sense of the word. This is an important distinction to make, because the recipes in this book are all about traditional barbecue, which is not the same thing as grilling.

Traditional barbecue is smoked, not grilled. It is cooked "low and slow," generally between 225°F and 275°F, and always flavored with wood smoke. When pitmasters talk about barbecuing meat, it is positioned a fair distance away from the fire, whether the fire is located below the cooking surface or off to the side, as when it is in a separate firebox. This method turns tough, chewy cuts of meat tender and juicy, which is why beef brisket, pork shoulder, and ribs are popular choices for traditional barbecue.

Grilling, on the other hand, involves cooking "hot and fast," at temperatures above 300°F. The fire is positioned directly beneath the cooking surface and quickly creates a hard sear on the surface of the meat. Grilling works well for tender cuts of meat such as steaks or chops as well as delicate fish and seafood. Anything that would only turn tough and dry when cooked for a long time is better suited for grilling.

▶ ESSENTIAL TOOLS AND EQUIPMENT

Certain tools and equipment should be on every aspiring pitmaster's shopping list. These are the bare essentials to get started, but for people who are looking to take things to the next level, see "The Pitmaster's Arsenal" in chapter 2.

Thermometers. Ideally, you'll have two different thermometers: one that will allow you to monitor the temperature of the cooking chamber at surface level, and one that will help you keep an eye on the internal temperature of the meat. For the first task, a simple oven thermometer will do. If your smoker has a built-in thermometer, you might want to use an oven thermometer to calibrate it, since built-ins sometimes give inaccurate readings. For the second task, look for an instant-read thermometer that can take the heat of the cooking compartment. When you start cooking, insert it into the meat and leave it there so you won't have to make a new hole (from which juices escape) every time you take a temperature reading.

Tongs. Look for sturdy, long-handled tongs that close fully. They should be easy for you to work with and long enough to isolate your hands from the heat of the smoker. Don't be tempted by self-locking tongs, which are gimmicky and difficult to use.

Shovel. This is a must-have if you're working with charcoal or wood, for stoking the fire and also cleaning out ash.

Squeeze bottle. Keep this handy to douse flare-ups.

Spice shaker. Use a spice shaker to apply rub evenly on meat.

Grill brush. This is the ideal tool for cleaning the cooking grates. You can either buy inexpensive ones often or invest in a nicer one that may last longer. Whatever you decide, check the brush after each use to make sure bristles haven't fallen out. You don't want them to end up in your food.

Timers. Consider purchasing several digital kitchen timers to help you keep track of your overall cook time as well as side dishes that are cooking simultaneously.

Cutting boards. The bigger the cutting board, the better, especially if you're working with large cuts of meat like pork shoulder and brisket. Have at least two on hand: a nonporous one that can be sanitized for trimming raw meat, and another one for slicing cooked meats.

Knives. Look for a high-quality chef's knife from a reputable manufacturer such as Henckels, Global, or Wüsthof. Make sure to pick a size that you are comfortable working with. Long-bladed slicing or serrated knives are also nice to have if you plan on slicing brisket or pork shoulder often.

Aluminum foil. If you plan on wrapping your meats during the cooking process, you'll need plenty of foil.

Disposable aluminum pans. These are useful for storing and carrying large cuts of cooked meat. They can also be used as a makeshift water pans or drip pans if your smoker isn't equipped with one.

Small kitchen towels. Use these to coat the cooking grates with oil.

Chimney starter. This device is the best and safest way to light charcoal if you're using a charcoal smoker. They're inexpensive and well worth the money.

Barbecue lighter. Designed with the pitmaster in mind, these lighters have long necks that allow you to light charcoal and wood fires with ease.

Fire extinguisher. This is a must-have for putting out any fire in your backyard or kitchen.

2

PREP

PREPARATIONS FOR THE PERFECT COOK

s any pitmaster will tell you, the key to a successful cook is preparation and planning. Of course, getting it right takes time, patience, and practice—hardly anyone nails a perfect brisket the first time—but having the right information and tools at your disposal can make it a whole lot easier to learn from your mistakes.

In this chapter, we'll walk you through meat selection, cooking techniques, and fuel sources. You'll learn about sourcing wood and the properties of the different types, and also get a quick rundown on stocking your pantry. Lastly, you'll find some general tips and advice on how to get the most out of every barbecue session, as well as specific pointers on how to take your skills to the next level and enter amateur competitions with your own signature style.

PICKING YOUR PROTEINS

Before barbecue became regionalized in the early twentieth century, people smoked all kinds of meat. Since barbecues were largely public gatherings that relied on food donations, pitmasters worked with whatever was available locally, and they cooked whole animals. Everything from pigs and sheep to oxen and opossums were a common sight.

Meat choices have narrowed down since then. The emergence of barbecue restaurants across the country combined with immigrant influences to create regional styles, resulting in preferences for certain animals and certain cuts of meat. Generally, they were the humbler cuts; tough and chewy, they required a lot of cooking to render them tender. These are the cuts that remain popular today for barbecue. So, thankfully, you don't need to spend a ton of money on expensive cuts of meat to create authentic 'cue.

▶ PORK

Pork is so ingrained in the barbecue traditions of many of the regions, it seems like a good place to start a discussion about meat. These are the traditional cuts used for barbecue:

Pork shoulder. The shoulder comes from the front of the animal and typically weighs from 12 to 18 pounds. Because of its size, it is often split by butchers into two smaller, roughly equal parts: the Boston butt and the picnic ham. Make sure to buy bone-in shoulders for the best flavor.

Boston butt. Confusingly, this doesn't come from the derrière of the animal, but rather the top part of the shoulder, where it sits above the picnic ham. It's also simply called "pork butt" at some stores. Compared to a picnic ham, this part has more collagen and meat.

Picnic ham. This is also a misnomer. This comes from the part just above the front leg, whereas normal ham comes from the rear end of the animal. It does taste more like ham than Boston butt, which may be where it got its name. Compared to a Boston butt, it has more bone and fat.

Baby back ribs. This popular cut comes from the top of the rib cage, just above the loin. Baby backs usually come pre-brined and packed in plastic, which is unfortunate since the brine adds water weight and preservatives. You'll likely run into the same problem with spareribs, so if you can find a butcher that doesn't sell them pre-packed, consider yourself lucky.

Spareribs. These are a hidden gem. Many professional pitmasters prefer these over baby backs because of their higher collagen and fat content, and this translates to better flavor. Spareribs come from the bottom part of the rib cage and are adjacent to the belly. When shopping for them, watch out for shiners, which are pieces of bone that jut out through the meat. Not only will you pay more for less meat, but they ruin the bark as the ribs cook.

> **HOG WILD**
> For North Carolinians, barbecue *is* pork, nothing else. And although their affinity for pork is well known, most don't know just how deep that love goes. For quite some time now, the state has had more hogs than people. According to John Shelton Reed, author of *Holy Smoke: The Big Book of North Carolina Barbecue*, Duplin County alone has more than two million hogs, or a ratio of 40 hogs per person.

St. Louis–style ribs. These are spareribs that have been squared off, making them easier to cook evenly.

Whole pig. Okay, so this is obviously not a cut. But the tradition of barbecue in America began with cooking whole pigs, so it makes sense to include it. So, what should you look for when buying a whole pig? Generally speaking, pitmasters get their pigs dressed and butterflied (with skin intact), which means all the hair, organs, feet, and tail have been removed, and the animal can be laid flat on the grates. As for how much to buy, 90 pounds is a good place to start. That will yield 20 to 30 pounds of meat. Look to your neighborhood butcher to point you in the right direction on where to buy one.

▶ BEEF

After pork, beef is arguably the next most popular choice for barbecue. Here are the traditional barbecue cuts:

Brisket. Brisket comes from the chest of a steer and usually weighs between 10 and 20 pounds. It consists of two parts—the flat and the point. The flat is the larger portion and the point is the triangular part sitting above it, which has more intramuscular fat and collagen and results in the famous "burnt ends." When buying brisket, make sure to get a packer-trimmed brisket so you get both parts, and try to pick one with a nice even flat. Avoid selecting ones with a lot of hard fat; you'll end up trimming it all off anyway, so it's money down the drain.

Beef ribs. Beef ribs come from three different parts of the animal—the chuck, the rib, and the plate. The chuck and rib are adjacent to each other and run along the top side, while the plate sits below and runs along the bottom. The best ribs for barbecue come from the plate; these have the most meat, intramuscular fat, and collagen. Beef ribs have tons of flavor and are a real treat.

▶ POULTRY

While for some it may not be as exciting as pork or beef, chicken and turkey certainly have their place in traditional barbecue. Here are your options:

Whole chicken. Because it is a small, lean animal, whole chickens work best for barbecue. When shopping for poultry, look for birds that have not been injected with brine. These artificially inflate the weight of the animal, and you end up paying for water. If you can find them, air-chilled birds have the best flavor; they're a little pricier but well worth the premium.

Whole turkey. A 12-pound turkey will serve approximately 12 people. As with chickens, avoid pre-brined birds when possible and opt for organic, wild, or heritage-breed birds if you can afford it.

Turkey breasts. When it comes to turkey, you can opt to use just the breasts if you're cooking for a small group of people. Make sure to get them bone-in.

▶ LAMB

Lamb and mutton were once popular choices for barbecue throughout the country, but now they are largely confined to the western reaches of Kentucky. These are the best cuts for barbecue:

Lamb shoulder. The shoulder is tough but has good flavor and turns tender as it slow cooks.

Leg of lamb. The leg is slightly more tender than the shoulder. Make sure to get this bone-in for maximum flavor.

FUEL FOR FIRE—AND FLAVOR

To create the heat needed to cook your barbecue, your smoker will run on one of three fuel sources, each with its pros and cons.

▶ CHARCOAL

There are two types of charcoal available today: charcoal briquettes and lump charcoal.

Charcoal briquettes are made from compressed hardwood. The best brands use cornstarch as a binder; cheaper ones are laced with chemicals. Briquettes are easy for beginners because they burn evenly (owing to their shape), making it easier to maintain a steady temperature. Avoid "self-starting" briquettes since they are coated with lighter fluid.

Lump charcoal is made by burning logs gradually until all the water and resin evaporates. They have no additives and burn hotter, which makes them a favorite of professional pitmasters, but they tend to crumble in the bag.

Charcoal itself doesn't add any flavor to the food, however. For that, you need to add hardwood chips or chunks to the fire to create smoke. Cleanup can be difficult, and you'll need to stand by to add more charcoal to the cooking chamber periodically.

▶ GAS

Propane comes in 20-pound tanks and is an economical fuel source. Gas smokers preheat quickly and maintain a steady temperature easily. However, as with charcoal, the fuel source doesn't add any smoky flavor by itself, so you'll need to add hardwood chips or chunks periodically.

▶ WOOD

If you're using a charcoal or gas smoker, finding wood to create smoke is easy: Home improvement stores and Amazon sell wood chips and chunks. But, if you have a wood-burning smoker, you're in for a challenge, because you'll need to source whole logs.

What Kind of Wood to Buy

Opt for hardwood varieties, and avoid resinous woods like pine, which impart a bitter taste to food. Here are some of the most popular types traditionally used for barbecue, along with suggested pairings:

- **APPLE** has a subtle sweetness that lends itself well to pork.
- **CHERRY** has a well-rounded sweetness that makes it a versatile companion for all kinds of meats.
- **PECAN** is slightly nutty, reminiscent of almond. It is popular with pork.
- **HICKORY** is assertive enough to stand up to beef but is also great with pork. It is the preferred 'cue wood along the East Coast.
- **OAK** is also great for beef and pork. It is a popular choice in Central Texas for smoked sausage and brisket.
- **MESQUITE** has a bold flavor that pairs well with beef. It is the wood of choice for West Texas "cowboy-style" barbecue.

Beyond finding a suitable species of wood for your protein, it's also important to consider the freshness. This is a case where fresher is not actually better. Freshly cut wood still has a lot of water in it, making it unpredictable to work with. It takes a very long time to heat up and creates smoke that doesn't taste good. Wood that has been allowed to age is the best bet.

At the other end of the spectrum, you also want to avoid really old wood because it burns too fast and doesn't generate much smoke at all. Ideally, you will be able to find wood somewhere in the happy medium, but if all you can get is freshly cut wood, you can season it yourself (read on for details).

An easy way to tell whether wood is freshly cut is to feel its heft. Does it seem heavy for its size? If so, it is most likely freshly cut. Another test is to hold it up to your ear and rap it. If it doesn't sound hollow, then it's freshly cut.

How to Find Wood

Where do you find wood? Well, believe it or not, most pitmasters start by looking through Craigslist. There is a fair amount of trial and error involved since, as you would expect, there are some unscrupulous people out there. Once you do find your go-to source, try to cultivate a relationship and make a point of buying wood regularly. Until then, though, learn the lingo (a cord of wood is a stack of logs that is 8 by 4 by 4 feet; a face cord is 8 by 4 by 1½ feet), inspect the cargo, and don't pay for anything up front.

Preparing the Wood

If you buy freshly cut wood, there is a way to make it suitable for barbecue, but it's going to take time. You'll have to season it, or let it dry out. To help the process along, split the wood into smaller pieces, which exposes more surface area to the air.

To split wood, use a maul and a chopping block. Place the log vertically on the block and stand with your legs shoulder-width apart. In one smooth motion, bring the maul down directly on the wood, and follow through (you shouldn't need to put your back into it). Repeat, and stack the wood in a dry area with plenty of sunlight. Depending on the weather, it can take a few weeks to a few months.

THE ORIGIN OF THE WORD BARBECUE

There are plenty of theories on where the word barbecue comes from, including the French term *barbe à queue*, which means "beard to tail." But according to Robert F. Moss, author of *Barbecue: The History of an American Institution*, the term was first used for the cooking apparatus employed by the Taíno tribe in the Caribbean, as well as the cooking technique. Their setup was very similar to modern-day pits.

PANTRY ITEMS AND KITCHEN STAPLES

A well-stocked pantry is important for creating rubs, sauces, and side dishes to complement your barbecue. This list of suggested items isn't intended to be exhaustive, but it is a good place to start.

▶ HERBS AND SPICES

Allspice, whole	Coriander, ground	Paprika, smoked
Ancho chile, ground	Cumin seeds	Paprika, sweet
Cayenne pepper	Guajillo chile, ground	Peppercorns, black
Chili powder	Mustard, ground	Peppercorns, white
Chipotle chile, ground	Nutmeg, whole	Red pepper flakes
Cinnamon, ground	Oregano, dried	Salt, kosher
Cloves, whole	Oregano, Mexican, dried	Sesame seeds, white

▶ OTHER PANTRY ESSENTIALS

Baking powder	Jalapeños	Sugar, brown
Baking soda	Ketchup	Sugar, granulated
Broth, beef	Lemons	Sugar, turbinado
Broth, chicken, low-sodium	Limes	Tomato paste, canned
Butter, unsalted, low-sodium	Mayonnaise	Tomatoes, crushed, canned
	Molasses, blackstrap, unsulphured	Tomatoes, diced, canned
Buttermilk	Mustard, Dijon	Vegetable oil
Cilantro	Mustard, yellow	Vinegar, apple cider
Coffee, instant	Olive oil, extra-virgin	Vinegar, distilled white
Garlic	Onions	Worcestershire sauce
Honey	Parsley, flat-leaf	

TIPS AND TRICKS FOR SUCCESS

Here are a few helpful tips and tricks that will help you master the art and craft of barbecue.

Stock up on fuel. Always have more wood, charcoal, or gas on hand than you think you're going to need. You don't want to run out of fuel in the middle of a cook. If you're burning wood logs, 100 to 150 logs is a safe bet; for charcoal, 70 to 80 pounds is a good amount to keep on hand; and if you're using gas, keep a spare 20-pound tank of propane around.

Don't cook cold meat. Always let meat come to room temperature before cooking. This promotes even cooking for large cuts, and it also shaves hours off the cooking time.

Let the rub do its magic. Apply dry rub to meat at least 1 hour before cooking. This will allow it to draw moisture to the surface and meld with it, which will help the meat absorb smoke and create a nice crust, or bark.

If you're lookin', it ain't cookin'. It may be an age-old barbecue cliché, but it couldn't be more true. Don't open the cooking compartment any more than is absolutely necessary. You add roughly 15 minutes of cooking time every time you do.

Probe carefully. There's a right way and a wrong way to stick a thermometer into a piece of meat. Avoid inserting it in multiple places as this will cause juices to escape. Instead, find the thickest part of the meat and insert the thermometer all the way in without touching any bone.

Anticipate the stall. When you're cooking a large cut of meat, you'll notice that at some point the internal temperature will seem to hit a wall. This can last for hours, causing most people to wonder if the meat is done cooking. First of all: It's not done cooking. Second of all: Don't worry, this is completely normal. There are various theories that attempt to explain why this happens, but the point is that it does happen, every time. Eventually, your meat will climb out of the stall and the temperature will resume climbing. Resist the urge to pull it out early.

Rest before slicing. It may be tempting to cut into your meat right after it comes out of the cooking chamber, but always let it rest for a while to allow the juices to redistribute. Otherwise, you'll end up throwing away all your hard work. Slice into it too early and all the juices will escape, leaving you with a hunk of dry meat. Depending on the cut of meat, it should rest for at least a half hour; a full hour is always a safe bet. More specifically, the rest times should be as follows:

PORK SHOULDER, BUTT, AND PICNIC HAM: 1 hour

SPARERIBS AND BABY BACK RIBS: ½ hour

WHOLE PORK LOIN: 1 hour

BRISKET AND BEEF RIBS: 1 hour

WHOLE CHICKEN AND TURKEY: 1 hour

TURKEY BREAST AND CORNISH GAME HEN: ½ hour

LAMB LEG AND SHOULDER: 1 hour

LAMB RIBS: ½ hour

Install a water/drip pan. If your smoker comes with one, keep it full of water at all times. This circulates moisture inside the cooking chamber and prevents the meat from drying out as it cooks. It also helps keep the temperature stable. If it doesn't have one, a disposable aluminum pan will do nicely. Position it underneath the cooking grate so that it doubles as a drip pan, preventing flare-ups and making cleanup easier.

Keep the charcoal and wood coming. Keep an eye on the temperature inside the cooking chamber and add fuel as necessary, or adjust the vents to maintain a steady heat.

THE PITMASTER'S ARSENAL

To take your skills to the next level, you've got to have the right equipment. Here are some suggestions for additions to your toolbox.

Basting brush or mop. This is a handy tool for applying glazes to meats as they cook or sauces toward the end of the cooking time. It's great for whole pigs.

Large nonreactive containers. If you want to experiment with brining or marinating large cuts, these are essential. Look for glass or food-grade plastic; avoid aluminum because it will react with acidic ingredients. If you have access to a restaurant supply store, Cambros are a popular choice among professional pitmasters.

Heat-resistant gloves. Look for silicone gloves that cover your arms. If you plan on working with brisket, pork shoulder, or other large cuts on a regular basis, these will make your life a lot easier. You'll be able to just pick them up and move them around during the cooking process instead of dealing with tongs, which can break the bark you've worked so hard to create.

Bear paws. These are lots of fun to use for pulling pork or chicken.

Remote-probe thermometer. This allows you to monitor the internal temperature of your meat as it cooks without having to open the cooking compartment. You can insert the probe through one of the vents in your cooker.

Digital scale. Look for a scale with at least a 10-pound capacity. You'll want to use it to weigh meat before and after cooking.

FUNDAMENTAL TECHNIQUES

Most of the cuts used for traditional barbecue still require a fair amount of prep before you can start cooking them. In barbecue, preparation is half the battle. Although you could just take meat straight from the store, season it, and pop it into the smoker, you won't get stellar results. You could have the perfect fire, smoke, and temperature all throughout the cooking process, but if you haven't prepped, well, then you've just wasted time. That's why learning how to prep correctly is the most important technique in barbecue. We'll outline the preparation techniques for each of the four main proteins.

▶ PORK

Pork Shoulder

Before you start cooking a whole pork shoulder—or its subprimal cuts, the Boston butt and the picnic ham—make sure to do the following:

1 **Remove any hard fat.** Run your hands over the surface of the meat, noting any areas of hard fat. You need to trim off these patches, as they will not render during cooking. To do this, insert the tip of a chef's knife into the center of the patch and shave with smooth strokes going in one direction, following the curve of the meat. Don't worry if you cut off a bit of the meat. Repeat, going in the other direction. Leave the soft fat alone.

2 **Coat with rub.** Use a spice shaker to coat the meat evenly all over and let stand for 1 hour. If you like, first coat the meat all over with a light slather (such as mustard) to help the rub stick.

Baby Back Ribs

There isn't much prep to do with ribs—just two simple steps:

1 **Remove excess fat.** Trim any hanging pieces of fat. There shouldn't be much, if any at all.

2 **Coat with rub.** Use a spice shaker to coat the ribs evenly all over and let stand for 1 hour. If you like, first coat the meat all over with a light slather (such as mustard) to help the rub stick.

Spareribs

If you've purchased St. Louis–style ribs, proceed right to the rub. If not, prepare your spareribs as follows:

1 **Separate the breastbone remains.** Place the ribs bone-side up on your cutting board with the curved length away from you. Starting at the end with the longest bones, run your finger along the top of the rack until you reach the fourth rib. Near there, you should feel a slight gap where there's cartilage. This is where the remaining part of the breastbone meets the ribs. Position your knife there and make a clean slice through the cartilage all the way down toward the ends of the first three ribs.

2 **Remove any excess meat and fat.** It's a good idea to create a smooth surface before cooking; any small pieces of meat or fat that stick out from the rest of the rack will probably burn. Cut off excess meat at the narrow end to make a nice, straight line. Starting from that end, you may see a good-size chunk of meat running along the rack, jutting out from the bone. If you see it, slice it off. Also, trim off any chunks of fat that are hanging off the rack.

3 **Square off the remaining edges.** Flip the rack over and trim off any excess meat or fat there to make straight lines along all the edges. Make sure the edges don't have any pieces of bone sticking out; if they do, remove them with your knife.

4 **Coat with rub.** Use a spice shaker to coat the ribs evenly all over and let stand for 1 hour. If you like, first coat the meat all over with a light slather (such as mustard) to help the rub stick.

Whole Pig

If you're doing a whole pig, have your butcher do all the prep for you; even the hardiest of pitmasters don't bother prepping one on their own. Order the whole pig dressed and butterflied, which means all the interesting bits have been removed (hair, organs, hooves, and tail) and the animal has been flattened to cook evenly.

▶ BEEF

Brisket

Make sure the brisket is well chilled before trimming it; you'll have an easier time working with it. Then follow these steps:

1 **Trim the fat cap.** The fat cap is the layer of fat that runs all along one side of the brisket. Try your best to trim it down to an even ¼-inch thickness.

2 **Remove any hard fat.** Run your hands over the surface of the brisket, noting any areas of hard fat. Pay particular attention to where the two parts of the brisket—the point, which is the smaller, triangular portion, and the flat, which is the larger, rectangular portion—meet, since there is always a huge chunk of hard fat there. Cut out that chunk, then trim off any patches of hard fat on the rest of the brisket; they will not render during cooking. To trim off a patch of hard fat, insert the tip of a chef's knife or butcher's knife into the center of the patch and shave with smooth strokes going in one direction, following the curve of the meat. Don't worry if you cut off a bit of the meat. Repeat, going in the other direction. Leave the soft fat alone.

3 **Square off the edges.** Trim all sides to make straight lines along all the edges. You will likely need to cut off some meat along with the fat to get nice lines.

4 **Coat with rub.** Use a spice shaker to coat the meat evenly all over and let stand for 1 hour. If you like, first coat the meat all over with a light slather (such as mustard) to help the rub stick.

Ribs

Beef ribs are one of the few cuts that don't require much prep. Here's all you have to do:

1 **Remove any excess fat.** Trim any hanging pieces of fat. There shouldn't be much, if any at all.

2 **Coat with rub.** Use a spice shaker to coat the ribs evenly all over and let stand for 1 hour. If you like, first coat the meat all over with a light slather (such as mustard) to help the rub stick.

Whole Chicken

Chicken is lean and doesn't have much collagen compared to pork and beef. This means that it has a tendency to dry out when smoked. To prevent this, chicken should be placed in a wet brine before cooking.

Wet brine is just a term for a saltwater solution. You can fancy it up with all kinds of herbs, spices, fruit juices, condiments, and sugar, but at its simplest, it's just salt and water. There is a range of ratios that tend to work best—between 12 and 16 parts water to 1 part salt. Saltier brines result in juicier flesh, but that flesh will also be firmer. (Think of the mouthfeel of a holiday ham.) If you're adding other liquids to the brine besides water, they should not factor into this calculation.

How does wet brining work? Brining relies on the process of osmosis, or the movement of water between two separate areas based on how much salt is in each area. What this means is that water tends to move toward areas where there is more salt, in order to achieve equilibrium.

So, when you place chicken in brine, initially the flesh releases water. However, the flesh also absorbs some of the salt and, eventually, some water is reabsorbed by the flesh, increasing its ability to retain moisture when cooked. If you've placed any other ingredients in the brine, it also carries those flavors with it. This process continues until equilibrium is achieved. It's worth noting that brining for longer periods has the same effect as increasing the amount of salt in the brine.

The actual process of brining is simple:

1 Heat the salt and water together with any other ingredients you're using until the salt dissolves.

2 Transfer to a heat-proof container and refrigerate until cool. (Never pour hot brine on cold meat; this creates a food safety issue.)

3 Pour the cool brine over the chicken in a suitable container and refrigerate for 3 to 5 hours.

4 Drain and discard the brine. Pat the chicken dry.

5 Season with rub as usual, but go easy on the salt.

Whole Turkey

You'll become very popular at Thanksgiving when your friends and family learn how fast you can cook a delicious bird. Here, you'll learn a technique known as spatchcocking, which is just another way of saying butterflying.

Spatchcocking allows you to cook the bird quickly because it flattens out the bird, thereby increasing the surface area of the meat. Because of the increased surface area, more smoke flavor penetrates the flesh, making it unnecessary to remove the skin (which would make for a very strange-looking Thanksgiving turkey, indeed). This technique can also be used for whole chickens:

1 Place the turkey breast-side down on a cutting board.

2 Using kitchen scissors, cut along both sides of the backbone and remove it.

3 Open up the turkey and use a sharp knife to make shallow cuts along the bone that runs down the center of the breast.

4 Flip over the bird and use both palms to press down on the breast until it cracks.

Brine the bird for even better results. An overnight brine is advisable since this is a larger animal than a chicken. Drain and pat dry as usual the following day and use a spice shaker to coat with rub all over.

Turkey Breast

Chances are you won't often need to cook a whole bird. Turkey breasts are sufficient to feed up to six people, and they're much easier to handle and prepare than a whole bird. Here's all you need to do:

1 **Remove the skin.** Just rip it all off with your hands; you don't even need to use a knife. Because it is much thicker than chicken skin, it hinders the brine (and later, the smoke) from penetrating the flesh.

2 **Brine.** Follow the steps on page 42 to make a brine and submerge the breast for at least 3 hours or up to overnight.

3 **Pat dry.** Remove the breast from the brine and pat dry.

4 **Coat with rub.** Use a spice shaker to coat the breast evenly all over and let stand for 1 hour. If you like, first coat the meat all over with a light slather (such as mustard) to help the rub stick.

Lamb

Whether you're preparing leg of lamb or the shoulder, the techniques are similar:

1   Remove any hard fat. Run your hands over the surface of the meat, noting any areas of hard fat. Trim off these patches, as they will not render during cooking. To do so, insert the tip of a chef's knife into the center of the patch and shave with smooth strokes going in one direction, following the curve of the meat. Don't worry if you cut off a bit of the meat. Repeat, going in the other direction. Leave the soft fat alone.

2   Soak in buttermilk. This step is optional. In Western Kentucky, folks like the sometimes gamey flavor of lamb, which pairs well with the region's traditional Black Barbecue Sauce (page 224). However, if you want to tone down the gaminess, buttermilk works wonders. Soak the meat and refrigerate for at least 3 hours or up to overnight, then drain and pat dry.

3   Coat with rub. Use a spice shaker to coat the meat evenly all over and let stand for 1 hour. If you like, first coat the meat all over with a light slather (such as mustard) to help the rub stick.

BEYOND THE BASICS: YOUR FIRST COOK-OFF

Once you've mastered the basics and have developed your 'cue chops, you can show off your newfound barbecuing skills to friends, family, and neighbors—and perhaps even participate in an amateur-level competition. As you continue to hone your barbecue skills, you'll begin to develop your own signature style.

▶ FIVE KEYS TO CROWD-WORTHY BARBECUE

If you keep these principles in mind, you'll find yourself cooking for a crowd with confidence.

Do a few trial runs. Focus on one protein that you find challenging and practice a few times before you serve it at a large gathering.

Take notes. Each time you cook it, take plenty of notes to learn from your mistakes. A sample worksheet is provided on page 46.

Budget your time generously. As a rule of thumb, figure on spending 1½ to 2 hours per pound of meat from start to finish. This range accounts for any time lost from opening the lid to check on temperatures and to baste. You should, of course, monitor the condition of your meat as it cooks since a number of factors can affect how long it takes to cook. But this should give you an idea of how much time you'll need on the big day and when you need to get started. Nothing is worse than having a crowd of hungry people waiting for you to finish cooking.

Figure out your portions. Unfortunately, one of the drawbacks of cooking low and slow is that you can't just put another rack of ribs in the cooker when you find out you're a few portions short. All meat shrinks when it cooks, but by different amounts depending on the cut and the amount of time spent cooking. So when you're doing your trial runs, make sure to record the raw weight and the cooked weight each time to obtain a yield. This will help you figure out how much to buy for the big day.

Don't be afraid to ask for help. There's a whole community of budding pitmasters out there just like you. Look to the Resources section for some great meat smoking forums to join.

▶ THE ABCs OF COMPETING IN ABCs (AMATEUR BARBECUE COMPETITIONS)

Here are some frequently asked questions about getting started in the competitive circuit.

How do I find a cook-off? Amateur competitions are usually organized by city organizations, such as the Chamber of Commerce; service organizations such as the Lions; and local charities and religious organizations.

Where are they held? A typical venue is a park, parking lot, or fairground. Organizers obtain permits for outdoor spaces in advance.

Are these competitions seasonal? It depends on where you live. In areas with snowy or rainy winters, you probably won't see too many competitions December through March.

Will I need special equipment? Generally, no, but if you find a competition that is sanctioned by one of the larger national organizations, they may have special rules about what kind of fuel you can burn, what kinds of meat you can cook, and so on.

▶ ADDING YOUR CREATIVE SPIN

Much of this book deals with the foundations of traditional barbecue. As you'll see in chapter 9, however, barbecue is continually evolving. In developing your signature style, use the fundamental techniques that you've learned from cooking your way through the recipes in this book, but don't be afraid to look outside of tradition for inspiration.

Experiment with different types of meat. The recipes in this book focus on the traditional proteins smoked throughout the different regions—namely, pork, beef, chicken, turkey, and lamb. But that shouldn't stop you from branching out and trying new things. How about duck, salmon, or oysters? Before barbecue became regionalized, Americans smoked all kinds of meats and seafood. There's no reason you can't follow in their footsteps.

WORKSHEET

DATE: PROTEIN: CUT:

WEIGHT BEFORE COOKING: WEIGHT AFTER COOKING:

PREP (butchering, brining, or marinating techniques and times):

RUB:

COOKING TEMPERATURE: COOKING TIME:

RESULTS (texture, flavor, level of juiciness, and other indicators of quality):

IDEAS FOR IMPROVEMENTS NEXT TIME:

Draw upon your own cooking experience. Much of what is considered "traditional" barbecue today actually owes its origins to immigrant traditions; they've just been ingrained for so long that most people don't realize it anymore. But if you've enjoyed Piedmont-style pork shoulder or Central Texas–style smoked sausage, you can thank German and Czech settlers for that. Those immigrants brought their long-standing traditions with them. The same goes for Memphis-style dry ribs: Enterprising Greek American restaurateurs came up with that style, which is why most dry rubs feature dried oregano as an ingredient. What culinary tradition do you come from, and what can you contribute to the evolution of barbecue?

Don't just cook—eat. Every once in a while, you've got to look up from the books and get out of your own kitchen. Experience as many different styles of barbecue as you can; travel far and wide if you can afford to do so. If you truly have a passion for barbecue, it will be well worth it.

Serve with flair. While there are plenty of recipes for sides and desserts scattered throughout the chapters of this book, when you get right down to it, most barbecue joints serve their 'cue one of two ways: as a sandwich or as a plate. But you can get so much more creative than that. Take a favorite dish and use barbecue as a way to enhance it. For example, think of the last time you had Vietnamese pho. Did you like the brisket that was in the soup? Chances are, if you're honest, it was pretty lackluster. Why not barbecue a brisket rubbed with ground star anise and cinnamon and create the ultimate version of pho?

Maintain a worksheet. One of the best ways to improve your technique is to take plenty of notes. Use the sample worksheet (page 46) to keep track of sessions.

TWO

A CROSS-SECTION
OF REGIONAL
CLASSICS

EARLY ROOTS

arbecue within
en a regional
at was cooked,
ay it was served,
lemented it.
a fairly recent
rly twentieth
s and the rise of
s we recognize
lemphis—began
ad undergone
first settlers
Native American
he next century,
west in search
increasingly
rise to a rich
ved today. These early roots of barbecue are the focus of this chapter.

PROTEINS

Whole animals were the name of the game, and they were cooked low and slow over a spit, basted by their own juices hitting the coals below. Whatever animals were plentiful in a region became the barbecue meat of choice there. For the Native Americans along the East Coast, it was often wild turkey and deer. In the Caribbean, whole hogs reigned supreme. And for the first settlers who arrived in Virginia, hogs were also the most popular choice, though the occasional sheep would also be served.

In the 1700s and 1800s, as more people migrated south into the Carolinas and Georgia, and west into Kentucky, Tennessee, and Texas, the choices of meat for a barbecue became even more varied—it was common to see oxen, goats, rabbits, and even squirrels.

FLAVORS, RUBS, AND SAUCES

Seasoning was simple: just salt and pepper. That tradition still persists today in some parts of the country, notably Central Texas, where beef brisket is usually seasoned with nothing else.

As for sauce, there was one sauce that was served throughout the country: a simple mixture of butter, vinegar, salt, cayenne, and black pepper. Cooked in large batches, it was mopped onto the animals as they cooked over the spit. Today, it is still served as a dipping sauce (minus the butter) for whole hog in Eastern North Carolina; food historians speculate that its origins lie in a Caribbean concoction made with wine and peppers.

FILL THE PLATE

Many of the side dishes associated with barbecue—and Southern cooking in general—originated from the cooking of African American slaves, who were often the pitmasters tending the fire when their masters hosted community gatherings. In addition, there were cooks who helped prepare the sides and desserts to make a complete meal. Many dishes originated from barbecues that slaves held for themselves during holidays such as Christmas. These dishes could be cooked simultaneously over the fire without too much trouble, so there were plenty of soups, stews, unleavened bread, baked beans, and simple pies.

POPULAR PAIRINGS

Rum and rough whiskey were the spirits that fueled many barbecues, which more often than not were rowdy affairs. Rum punch was particularly popular, for which you'll find a recipe in this chapter.

POINTS TO REMEMBER

★ **Charcoal safety.**
If you're using a chimney starter to light a charcoal fire, always light it over the charcoal grate of your smoker, another grill, or other non-combustible surface, such as a terra-cotta pot (without a drainage hole) or fireproof bricks. Avoid lighting over concrete, which could shatter and cause injury.

★ **Baste every halftime.**
When basting, it's best to hold off for the first half of the cooking time, which is when the meat absorbs the most smoke. After this, basting helps keep the surface moist and continues to attract smoke. As time passes, you'll need to baste more often. A good rule of thumb is to baste every time another half of the remaining cooking time has passed. So, for a protein that takes about 8 hours to cook, you'll baste after 4 hours, and again 2 hours later, 1 hour later, and once more half an hour later.

★ **Spatchcocking? Have the right tools.** Spatchcocking, or butterflying, poultry is an easy technique to master, as long as you have a good pair of poultry shears and a very sharp knife.

★ **Giblets, be gone.** When cooking a whole turkey or chicken, don't forget to remove the giblets and other organs, which can usually be found in a bag in the cavity. Note that turkeys sometimes have bags in both the main cavity and the neck cavity.

★ **Don't pig out alone.**
Planning on tackling a whole hog? It's definitely a two-person job. From carrying the hog to flipping it over during the cooking process and picking it apart when it's done, you'll be glad you had a friend to help you out.

VIRGINIA-STYLE BARBECUED LAMB

★ PREP TIME: 1 HOUR ★

COOK TIME: 7½ TO 9 HOURS, PLUS 1 HOUR TO REST

Style: **EARLY VIRGINIAN**

SERVES 12 Although whole pigs were the most commonly cooked animals in the early days of barbecue, lamb or mutton would also make an appearance from time to time.

1 (5- to 6-pound) bone-in leg of lamb
2 tablespoons kosher salt
2 tablespoons freshly ground black pepper
1 cup Basic Basting Sauce (page 67)
Vegetable oil, for brushing the grates

⭐ *Soaking the lamb in buttermilk overnight helps cut down on any gamey flavors.*

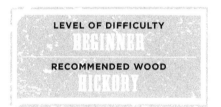

LEVEL OF DIFFICULTY
BEGINNER

RECOMMENDED WOOD
HICKORY

1 Trim the lamb and season it with the salt and pepper (see page 44). Let it stand at room temperature for 1 hour.

2 Preheat the smoker to 225°F to 275°F.

3 If using wood chips or chunks, soak them in water for at least 15 to 30 minutes. Add them to the smoker following the manufacturer's instructions.

4 Oil the grates and place the lamb on them, fat-side up. Close the cooking compartment and smoke for 7 ½ to 9 hours, basting every halftime (after about 4 hours, 2 hours later, 1 hour later, and ½ hour later), or until an instant-read thermometer inserted without touching the bone reads 190°F. Add wood and fuel as necessary to maintain the smoke and temperature in the smoker.

5 Remove the lamb from the smoker and let it rest for 1 hour. Discard any bones and slice or chop the meat before serving.

SMOKED WILD TURKEY

★ **PREP TIME: 1 HOUR, PLUS OVERNIGHT TO BRINE** ★
COOK TIME: 2 TO 2½ HOURS, PLUS 1 HOUR TO REST

Style: EARLY AMERICAN

SERVES 9   Wild turkeys roamed the woods of the first colonies and frontier settlements, and these heritage breeds are making a comeback today. Their flavor is comparable to dark turkey meat.

FOR THE BRINING LIQUID
1 gallon water
2 cups kosher salt

FOR THE TURKEY
1 (9- to 10-pound) wild turkey
2 tablespoons kosher salt
6 tablespoons freshly ground black pepper
Vegetable oil, for brushing the grates

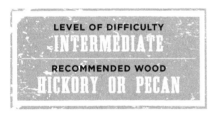 *Wild turkey can be ordered online from specialty purveyors such as D'Artagnan (www.dartagnan.com), or your local butcher.*

LEVEL OF DIFFICULTY
INTERMEDIATE
RECOMMENDED WOOD
HICKORY OR PECAN

TO MAKE THE BRINING LIQUID
In a large pot, heat the water and salt until the salt dissolves. Cool completely.

TO MAKE THE TURKEY
1 In a nonreactive container, submerge the turkey in the brine and refrigerate it overnight.

2 Remove the turkey from the brine and pat it dry. Spatchcock the turkey and season it with the salt and pepper (see page 43). Let it stand at room temperature for 1 hour.

3 Preheat the smoker to 225°F to 275°F.

4 If using wood chips or chunks, soak them in water for at least 15 to 30 minutes. Add them to the smoker following the manufacturer's instructions.

5 Oil the smoker grates and place the turkey on them, skin-side up. Close the cooking compartment and smoke the turkey for 2 to 2 ½ hours, or until an instant-read thermometer inserted without touching the bone reads 165°F. Add wood and fuel as necessary to maintain the smoke and temperature in the smoker.

6 Remove the turkey from the smoker and let it rest for 1 hour. Carve off the breasts, thighs, and legs and serve.

CARIBBEAN-STYLE SMOKED WHOLE HOG

★ **PREP TIME: 1 HOUR** ★
COOK TIME: 9 TO 12 HOURS, PLUS 1 HOUR TO REST

Style: CARIBBEAN

SERVES 30   In *The Barbacue Feast: Or, The Three Pigs of Peckham,* Edward Ward tells the tale of a group of traveling Englishmen who encounter barbecue for the first time in Jamaica in the 1700s. Drunk on rum, they sober up on "a Litter of Pigs nicely cook'd after the West Indian manner," which apparently involved "a most admirable Composition of Green Virginia Pepper and Madeira wine . . . daubed on with a Fox's Tail." This recipe is inspired by that account. Note that you'll need 75 to 85 pounds of charcoal for this project.

FOR THE BASTING LIQUID
2 (750-milliliter) bottles Madeira wine
1 green bell pepper, seeded and chopped
5 jalapeños, seeded and chopped

FOR THE HOG
1 (90-pound) hog, dressed and butterflied
Kosher salt
Freshly ground black pepper
Vegetable oil, for brushing the grates

⭐ *The dog bone pattern (like a capital letter I) places more heat underneath the shoulders and hams, which take longer to cook, and less heat underneath the loin and ribs, which cook more quickly.*

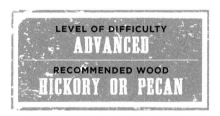

LEVEL OF DIFFICULTY
ADVANCED
RECOMMENDED WOOD
HICKORY OR PECAN

TO MAKE THE BASTING LIQUID
In a large pot, combine the wine, bell pepper, and jalapeños. Cook over high heat until the wine is reduced by about half. Set aside.

TO MAKE THE HOG
1 Season the hog generously with salt and pepper. Let it stand at room temperature for 1 hour.

2 If using wood chunks, soak them in water for at least 15 to 30 minutes.

3 Light 25 to 30 pounds of charcoal using chimney starters (see page 20), then spread them in a dog bone pattern along the bottom of your smoker. Once all the coals turn gray and the smoker reaches 225°F to 250°F, add the wood (if using) near the coals to create smoke.

➤➤

⇒ CARIBBEAN-STYLE SMOKED WHOLE HOG

4 Oil the smoker grates and place the hog on them, skin-side up. Close the cooking compartment and smoke the hog for 6 to 8 hours, basting it every halftime with the liquid, or until an instant-read thermometer inserted into the shoulders and hams without touching the bone reads 165°F. Add wood and fuel underneath the two ends of the pig as necessary to maintain the smoke and temperature in the smoker, and push cooler embers toward the center.

5 With the help of another person, grasp the two ends of the pig with heat-resistant gloves and flip it over. It may fall apart a bit, which is fine.

6 Pour the remaining basting liquid all over the pig. Cook for 3 to 4 more hours, or until the shoulders and hams reach an internal temperature of 180°F.

7 Remove the hog from the grates and let it rest for 1 hour, or until it is cool enough to handle with bare hands.

8 Pick the meat apart using your hands, or separate it into large chunks and chop or pull the meat.

VIRGINIAN BRUNSWICK STEW

PREP TIME: 10 MINUTES ★ **COOK TIME: 1 HOUR**

Style: EARLY VIRGINIAN

SERVES 6   Brunswick stew is a popular side in North Carolina and Georgia today, but its origins lie in colonial Virginia. The very first recorded recipes for Brunswick stew call for squirrel, but since those are pretty hard to get these days (not to mention illegal, in most states), this reimagined version uses chicken thighs instead. By all accounts, squirrels are a bit stringy, anyway.

3 bacon slices

2 large white or yellow onions, diced

2 pounds boneless, skinless chicken thighs, diced

8 cups cubed stale bread

8 cups water

½ cup (1 stick) unsalted butter

1 tablespoon kosher salt

1 tablespoon freshly ground black pepper

⭐ *Day-old baguettes, French bread, or Italian loaves work best for this recipe.*

1 In a large pot, cook the bacon over high heat for 1½ to 2 minutes, or until crisp on one side. Reduce the heat to medium, flip the bacon, and cook the other side for 1 to 2 minutes. Remove the bacon and set it aside. Do not drain the rendered fat from the pot.

2 Increase the heat under the pot to medium-high, add the onions, and cook them until slightly softened, 6 to 7 minutes.

3 Add the chicken, bread, water, butter, salt, and pepper to the pot and bring the water to a simmer. Crumble the bacon into the pot. Cook the stew for 45 minutes to 1 hour, stirring occasionally, or until it reaches a stew consistency. Serve immediately.

SOUTHERN-STYLE TURNIP GREENS

PREP TIME: 10 MINUTES ★ **COOK TIME: 35 MINUTES**

Style: EARLY AMERICAN

SERVES 4   In the early days of our country, turnip greens were a very popular side dish to serve at a typical barbecue. Some barbecue joints in the South still serve them today.

3 bacon slices

2 bunches turnip greens, coarsely chopped

¾ cup low-sodium chicken broth

1 cup diced canned tomatoes, drained

2 tablespoons distilled white vinegar

2 tablespoons light brown sugar

Kosher salt

Freshly ground black pepper

★ *Look for turnip greens that are bright green and springy to the touch. Avoid bunches with limp or yellowing leaves.*

1 In a large pot, cook the bacon over high heat for 1½ to 2 minutes, or until crisp on one side. Reduce the heat to medium, turn the bacon, and cook the other side for 1 to 2 minutes. Remove the bacon and set it aside. Do not drain the rendered fat from the pot.

2 Reduce the heat to medium-low and add the turnip greens, chicken broth, tomatoes, vinegar, and sugar to the pot. Season them with salt and pepper. Cover and cook for 30 minutes, or until tender.

3 Divide the greens among four plates, crumble the bacon on top, and serve immediately.

ANTEBELLUM CORNBREAD

PREP TIME: 10 MINUTES ★ **COOK TIME: 30 MINUTES**

Style: EARLY AMERICAN

SERVES 6   In the pre–Civil War era, cornbread was a bit different than it is today. It was unleavened and had no sugar, and it was often cooked in a skillet right over the ashes of a fire. This version makes practical use of an oven but in all other respects remains as honest (and dense) as the original.

Cooking spray

1½ cups finely ground white cornmeal

1 teaspoon kosher salt

1¾ cups water

2 tablespoons bacon fat, melted

⭐ *An interesting variation to try is to boil the water before adding it to the cornmeal, which, some insist, gives the bread a smoother texture.*

1 Preheat the oven to 375°F. Coat an 8-inch square baking dish or 9-inch cast iron skillet with cooking spray.

2 In a medium bowl, mix together the cornmeal and salt. Stir in the water, followed by the melted bacon fat.

3 Transfer the mixture to the baking dish or skillet and bake it for 30 minutes, or until golden brown on top.

OLD-SCHOOL MACARONI AND CHEESE

PREP TIME: 10 MINUTES ★ **COOK TIME: 35 MINUTES**

Style: **EARLY AMERICAN**

SERVES 8 When Thomas Jefferson and mac 'n' cheese first met, we're pretty sure he said something along the lines of "Where have you been all my life?" It's certainly a favorite comfort food of many Americans even today.

1 teaspoon kosher salt, plus more for the boiling water

2½ cups dried macaroni

4 tablespoons unsalted butter

5 tablespoons all-purpose flour

3 cups milk, warmed

Pinch cayenne pepper

1 teaspoon freshly ground white pepper

12 ounces grated Parmesan

1 cup seasoned bread crumbs

★ *Nutmeg is also a nice addition to the sauce; try swapping a pinch of it for the cayenne.*

1 Preheat the oven to 350°F.

2 Bring a large pot of salted water to a boil over high heat. Add the macaroni and boil it for 5 minutes, or until it is al dente, and drain it.

3 Meanwhile, in a large ovenproof skillet, melt the butter over medium heat. Whisk the flour into the butter, making sure no lumps form, for 3 to 5 minutes, or until the mixture is light brown. Stir the milk into the mixture and bring it to a boil. Reduce the heat to a simmer and whisk continuously until the sauce coats the back of a spoon.

4 Season the cheese sauce with the cayenne, salt, and white pepper and stir in the macaroni and cheese. Top the mac 'n' cheese with the bread crumbs and bake for 15 to 20 minutes, or until the top browns. Serve immediately.

SWEET POTATO PIE

PREP TIME: 10 MINUTES ★ COOK TIME: 1½ HOURS

Style: EARLY AMERICAN

SERVES 8 Sweet potato pie is considered more of a dessert item today, but it began as a savory accompaniment to the smoked meat when African American slaves held barbecues on holidays such as the Fourth of July and Christmas.

2 pounds sweet potatoes, peeled and cut into 1-inch cubes

1 tablespoon vegetable oil

½ cup (1 stick) unsalted butter, at room temperature

3 large eggs, beaten

1 cup milk

1 tablespoon kosher salt

1 teaspoon freshly ground black pepper

1 store-bought pie shell

⭐ *The terms yams and sweet potatoes are used interchangeably at most supermarkets in the United States.*

1 Preheat the oven to 500°F.

2 In a large bowl, toss the potatoes with the vegetable oil. Arrange them on a baking sheet in a single layer. Roast the potatoes for 25 minutes, or until they are fork tender and golden brown around the edges. Remove them from the oven and return them to the large bowl. Reduce the oven temperature to 375°F.

3 Add the butter to the bowl with the potatoes and mash them together until smooth. Stir in the eggs, milk, salt, and pepper until they are fully incorporated. Transfer the mixture to the pie shell.

4 Bake the pie for 1 hour, or until a toothpick inserted into the center comes out clean. Let the pie cool before slicing and serving.

MAPLE BAKED BEANS

★ PREP TIME: 5 MINUTES, PLUS OVERNIGHT TO SOAK ★
COOK TIME: 2 HOURS

Style: NEW ENGLAND

SERVES 8 Contrary to popular belief, baked beans didn't come from the South, but rather New England, where Native Americans once cooked it with maple syrup and bear fat. Bear fat is a little hard to come by, so this recipe uses bacon fat instead.

2½ cups dried navy beans

¼ cup bacon fat

1½ cups pure maple syrup

2 cups canned diced tomatoes, drained

2 tablespoons kosher salt

⭐ *Soaking dried beans overnight before cooking helps them cook faster.*

1 Put the beans in a large bowl, cover with water, and set aside at room temperature to soak overnight.

2 Drain the beans, transfer them to a large ovenproof pot, and cover with fresh water by 2 inches. Bring the water to a boil, reduce the heat to a simmer, and cook the beans for 30 to 35 minutes, or until they are tender. Drain the water from the beans.

3 Preheat the oven to 350°F.

4 Return the beans to the pot and add the bacon fat, maple syrup, diced tomatoes, and salt. Stir well to mix everything together and melt the bacon fat. Bake the beans, covered, for 70 to 80 minutes, or until they absorb the flavor of the cooking liquid.

BASIC BASTING SAUCE

PREP TIME: 5 MINUTES ★ **COOK TIME: 10 MINUTES**

Style: EARLY AMERICAN

MAKES ABOUT 1½ CUPS   Until barbecue became regionalized in the early twentieth century, "barbecue sauce" stuck to this basic formula, which dates back to the time of the first settlers. Whether you were in the Carolinas, Texas, or Tennessee, the same sauce was used to baste meats as they cooked over coals.

1 cup (2 sticks) unsalted butter
½ cup apple cider vinegar
2 tablespoons kosher salt
1 tablespoon red pepper flakes

⭐ *Butter can absorb off odors from other foods in the refrigerator. To keep it fresh, wrap any unused portions tightly in plastic wrap, and store it in a separate compartment.*

1 In a small pot, combine the butter, vinegar, salt, and red pepper flakes. Cook over medium heat, stirring occasionally, just until the butter is melted and the salt has dissolved, about 10 minutes.

2 Store the sauce in an airtight container in the refrigerator for up to a week.

HOT 'N' SPICY
SOUTH CAROLINA RUB

PREP TIME: 5 MINUTES ★ **COOK TIME: 10 MINUTES**

Style: EARLY SOUTH CAROLINA

MAKES ABOUT ½ CUP Although most accounts of barbecue prior to the Mexican-American War (1846–1848) speak of simple seasoning (if any at all), in South Carolina settlers got a jump start on spicing up their barbecue. Try this rub on just about anything you'd like to spice up.

2 teaspoons yellow mustard seeds

1 teaspoon black peppercorns

1 tablespoon smoked Spanish paprika

1 tablespoon sweet Spanish paprika

2 teaspoons cayenne pepper

1 teaspoon turbinado sugar

⅓ cup kosher salt

⭐ *Although early settlers probably wouldn't have gone to the trouble, toasting the whole spices in this recipe really brings out their flavor and aroma.*

1 In a small sauté pan, toast the yellow mustard seeds and black peppercorns over medium heat for 1 to 2 minutes, or until fragrant. Let them cool before blending thoroughly in a spice grinder. Transfer these ground spices to a small bowl.

2 Add the smoked paprika, sweet paprika, cayenne, sugar, and salt. Mix thoroughly. Keep in a sealed airtight container in a cool, dark place for up to 1 year.

GINGER CAKE

PREP TIME: 10 MINUTES ★ **COOK TIME: 1 HOUR**

Style: EARLY AMERICAN

SERVES 8 Ginger cake was often part of the spread at barbecues held by African American slaves in the Deep South up until the Civil War.

1 cup (2 sticks) unsalted butter, cubed, plus more for greasing the pan, all at room temperature

2½ cups all-purpose flour

2½ teaspoons baking powder

1 teaspoon kosher salt

1⅔ cups turbinado sugar

4 large eggs

½ cup milk

4 teaspoons ground ginger

⭐ *Always bring butter and eggs to room temperature before starting a baking recipe.*

1 Preheat the oven to 350°F.

2 Butter a 9-inch round springform or cake pan with 3-inch-high sides, and line the bottom of the pan with parchment paper.

3 In a medium bowl, mix together the flour, baking powder, and salt.

4 In the bowl of an electric mixer, cream 1 cup of butter and the sugar on medium speed for 3 minutes. Reduce the speed to medium-low and add the eggs one at a time; continue mixing for 1 to 2 minutes, or until the mixture is light tan in color.

5 With the mixer still running, add the milk and ginger. Then add the flour mixture, scraping down the sides as needed, until fully incorporated.

6 Transfer the batter to the prepared pan and bake the cake for 1 hour, or until a toothpick inserted into the center comes out clean. Let the cake cool before slicing and serving.

MOLASSES CAKE

PREP TIME: 10 MINUTES ★ COOK TIME: 30 MINUTES

Style: EARLY AMERICAN

SERVES 8 Molasses cake was another popular dessert at antebellum barbecues, devised as a way to make use of ingredients that were readily available.

⅔ cup unsalted butter, plus more for
  greasing the pan, all at room temperature
1½ cups all-purpose flour
1½ teaspoons baking powder
1 teaspoon kosher salt
1 cup unsulphured blackstrap molasses
½ cup milk
1 large egg

⭐ *To update this recipe for modern-day tastes, feel free to add some cinnamon, nutmeg, and ground ginger.*

1 Preheat the oven to 375°F.

2 Butter a 9-inch round springform or cake pan and line the bottom of the pan with parchment paper.

3 In a medium bowl, mix together the flour, baking powder, and salt.

4 In the bowl of an electric mixer, cream ⅔ cup of butter and the molasses, milk, and egg on medium speed for 3 minutes. On low speed, add the flour mixture, scraping down the sides as needed, until fully incorporated.

5 Transfer the batter to the prepared pan and bake the cake for 30 minutes, or until a toothpick inserted into the center comes out clean. Let the cake cool before slicing and serving.

RUM PUNCH

Style: EARLY AMERICAN

SERVES 8 A barbecue in the early days just wasn't the same without a little—or a lot of—rum punch.

3 cups light rum
2 cups pineapple juice
2 cups freshly squeezed orange juice
1 cup freshly squeezed lime juice
2 cups grenadine
10 dashes Angostura bitters

In a pitcher or punch bowl, combine all the ingredients. Place the pitcher in the refrigerator until thoroughly chilled.

⭐ *When juicing citrus fruits, firmly roll them beneath your palm on the countertop before cutting them in half. This will help them release more juice.*

THE CAROLINAS

According to food historians John and Dale Reed, North Carolina is home to the oldest continuous barbecue tradition in America. It's no wonder, then, that when it comes to barbecue, the regional rivalry within the state—between the Piedmont and Eastern North Carolina—can be fierce. ★ South Carolina has regional divisions as well, which mostly echo the north. But in the central part of the state, one finds a tradition that is unique to South Carolina: mustard sauce. ★ To an outsider, the debate over whose barbecue is "best" can seem overly intense. After all, it really just boils down to a few things: whether to serve the whole hog or just part of it, what kind of sauce it deserves, and, if you're really fanatical, what goes into the slaw. ★ There is one thing that everyone in the Carolinas can agree on, though: Only pork deserves to be called barbecue.

PROTEINS

Barbecue joints serve either whole hogs or shoulders. In Eastern North Carolina, it's always been about the whole hog, served either pulled or roughly chopped. In the Piedmont, you'll find smoked pork shoulder, served sliced, pulled, or chopped—a tradition that dates back to World War I, when a large number of German Americans settled in the area and started selling barbecue. And in South Carolina, the east-west divisions continue roughly along the same lines.

No matter where you go, though, the traditional way of barbecuing is the same: low and slow in a pit directly over a bed of coals, mopped with a basting sauce. The sauce and the juices from the meat hit the coals, creating smoke that's absorbed by the meat as it cooks. The coals are made by burning down hickory and sometimes oak in a time-consuming process. There are only a few restaurants that still cook this way, and those numbers are dwindling, as more and more turn to gas-fired burners for convenience.

FLAVORS, RUBS, AND SAUCES

When it comes to seasoning, Carolina pitmasters tend to stick to a simple mixture of salt and pepper. The sauce is where it gets interesting, though.

In North Carolina, pork is served with a thin, vinegar-based sauce. In the eastern part of the state, it consists of cider vinegar, salt, red pepper flakes, and black pepper—occasionally with a bit of sugar. In the Piedmont, tomato, usually in the form of ketchup, is added to the mix, often with a bit of sugar. This version of the sauce was popularized by German immigrants, who may have preferred the sweet-sour flavor profile that was common in the traditional dishes from their home country.

In South Carolina, the German influence crops up again, but in the form of mustard. In the central part of the state, you'll find sauces that use mustard together with honey or brown sugar to create a sweet-sour flavor profile. In the western part, ketchup creeps in; in the northwestern part, tomato; and in the eastern part, straight vinegar and pepper.

FILL THE PLATE

Slaw is a must-have with barbecue, of course, and regional variations abound. In Eastern North Carolina, dressings are mayonnaise-based and sweet, although some restaurants are also known to serve sinus-clearing mustard-based sauces, too. In the Piedmont, the tomato-based barbecue sauce often doubles as a dressing for slaw. And in between, the ketchup and mayonnaise have been known to meet. Other popular sides include Cornbread (page 94), Hushpuppies (page 83), North Carolina Brunswick Stew (page 85), and, in the south, Pulled Pork Hash (page 91) served over white rice. If dessert is served, chances are it'll be Peach Cobbler (page 101) or Banana Pudding (page 99).

POPULAR PAIRINGS

Sweet tea offers a natural contrast to vinegar-based sauces, making it a favorite beverage choice. Pepsi, invented in New Bern, North Carolina, is another popular choice in the eastern part, while Cheerwine, a cherry-flavored drink, is the soda of choice in the Piedmont. For something boozy, Tyson Ho, owner of Arrogant Swine, offers a twist on a classic cocktail, the Carolina Cherry Bounce (page 103).

POINTS TO REMEMBER

★ **Need a quick burst of heat?** If you're using a charcoal smoker, a drop in temperature inside the cooking compartment can be counteracted without requiring you to light fresh coals. Use a shovel to agitate the coals a bit, which will brush aside ash-covered pieces and stoke the fire.

★ **Perfect timing.** If the cooking compartment temperature starts to dip again toward the low end of the recommended range in the recipe, and the shovel trick doesn't cut it, it's time to light a fresh batch of coals.

★ **Use the right wood.** To replicate the flavor of authentic Carolina barbecue, seek out hickory or oak.

★ **Aim for the right temperatures.** Pork shoulders (including the butt and picnic) should be cooked to 185°F if slicing or chopping or 190°F if pulling; the same goes for the ham in the rear of the pig. Loins can be cooked to a range of temperatures from 135°F to 150°F; 140°F is medium.

★ **Wishful thinking.** If you're cooking a whole hog, arrange the coals in a dog bone pattern underneath, giving the shoulder and ham more heat and the loin and ribs less heat.

SMOKED PICNIC HAM

★ PREP TIME: 30 MINUTES ★
COOK TIME: 9½ TO 10½ HOURS, PLUS 1 HOUR TO REST

Style: PIEDMONT

SERVES 12   Sliced or chopped pork shoulder is what Piedmont barbecue is all about. For beginners, this part of the pork shoulder is a forgiving cut. You're more likely to have success in your first forays into barbecue, which will only whet your appetite to perfect your technique and move on to other cuts.

1 (7- to 8-pound) bone-in picnic ham
3 tablespoons kosher salt
3 tablespoons freshly ground black pepper
Vegetable oil, for brushing the grates

⭐ *If the cooking compartment gets too hot, close the vents on your cooker, thus cutting off the oxygen supply, to cool it off.*

LEVEL OF DIFFICULTY
BEGINNER

RECOMMENDED WOOD
HICKORY

1 Trim the ham and season it with the salt and pepper (see page 39). Let the ham stand at room temperature for 1 hour.

2 Preheat the smoker to 225°F to 275°F.

3 If using wood chips or chunks, soak them in water for at least 15 to 30 minutes. Add them to the smoker following the manufacturer's instructions.

4 Oil the smoker grates and place the ham on them. Close the cooking compartment and cook the ham for 7 to 7½ hours, or until an instant-read thermometer inserted without touching the bone reads 165°F. At this point, you may choose to wrap the ham in aluminum foil if you are concerned it will lose too much moisture as it continues to cook. Add wood and fuel as necessary to maintain the smoke and temperature in the smoker.

5 Turn over the ham and continue cooking for 2½ to 3 hours more, or until the internal temperature reaches 185°F.

6 Remove the ham from the smoker, discard the foil (if used), and let it rest for 1 hour. Discard the bones and slice or chop the meat. Be sure to mix in the crispy exterior with the meat when serving.

SMOKED PORK SHOULDER

★ PREP TIME: 30 MINUTES ★
COOK TIME: 9½ TO 10½ HOURS, PLUS 1 HOUR TO REST

Style: PIEDMONT

SERVES 24 Once you've successfully tackled part of a pork shoulder, you'll easily be able to take on the whole thing. Just remember that the same principles are at work here: low and slow with a steady supply of smoke.

1 (14- to 16-pound) bone-in whole
   pork shoulder
6 tablespoons kosher salt
6 tablespoons freshly ground black pepper
Vegetable oil, for brushing the grates

⭐ *Most butchers carry the shoulder already split into its two parts: the Boston butt and the picnic ham. If you want a whole one, you can special order it, or you can buy each part separately and just cook them together.*

LEVEL OF DIFFICULTY
INTERMEDIATE

RECOMMENDED WOOD
HICKORY

1 Trim the shoulder and season it with the salt and pepper (see page 39). Let it stand at room temperature for 1 hour.

2 Preheat the smoker to 225°F to 275°F.

3 If using wood chips or chunks, soak them in water for at least 15 to 30 minutes. Add them to the smoker following the manufacturer's instructions.

4 Oil the grates and place the shoulder on them. Close the cooking compartment and cook the meat for 7 to 7½ hours, or until an instant-read thermometer inserted without touching the bone reads 165°F. At this point, you may choose to wrap the meat in aluminum foil if you are concerned it will lose too much moisture as it continues to cook. Add wood and fuel as necessary to maintain the smoke and temperature in the smoker.

5 Turn over the shoulder and continue cooking for 2½ to 3 hours more, or until the internal temperature reaches 190°F.

6 Remove the shoulder from the smoker, discard the foil (if used), and let it rest for 1 hour. Discard the bones and pull or chop the meat. Be sure to mix in the crispy exterior with the meat when serving.

EASTERN NORTH CAROLINA SMOKED WHOLE HOG

★ **PREP TIME: 1 HOUR** ★
COOK TIME: 9 TO 12 HOURS, PLUS 1 HOUR TO REST

Style: **EASTERN NORTH CAROLINA**

SERVES 30 Traditionally, in Eastern North Carolina, a whole hog is cooked in a pit directly over coals, the idea being that any juices or fat will drip onto the hot coals and vaporize, thereby basting and flavoring the meat. This isn't terribly practical at home, but using a large smoker with charcoal and wood chunks—especially if you use hickory, which is the classic choice for this style—gives you nearly the same great flavor. Be generous with the salt and pepper seasoning since a lot of it will fall off during cooking. And remember—this is definitely at least a two-person job, so get your friends to help out! You'll need 75 to 85 pounds of charcoal for the entire barbecue process.

1 (90-pound) hog, dressed and butterflied
Kosher salt
Freshly ground black pepper
Vegetable oil, for brushing the grates
3 cups Vinegar–Red Pepper Sauce (page 97)

⭐ *Placing the hog on chicken wire before putting it onto the grates can make it easier to flip.*

LEVEL OF DIFFICULTY
ADVANCED
RECOMMENDED WOOD
HICKORY

1 Season the hog generously with salt and pepper. Let it stand at room temperature for 1 hour.

2 If using wood chunks, soak them in water for at least 15 to 30 minutes.

3 Light 25 to 30 pounds of charcoal using chimney starters (see page 20), then spread them in a dog bone pattern along the bottom of your smoker. Once all the coals turn gray and the smoker reaches about 225°F to 250°F, add the wood (if using) near the coals to create smoke.

➽

➤ EASTERN NORTH CAROLINA SMOKED WHOLE HOG

4 Oil the smoker grates and place the hog on them, skin-side up. Close the cooking compartment and smoke the hog for 6 to 8 hours, basting it every halftime with the Vinegar–Red Pepper Sauce, or until an instant-read thermometer inserted into the shoulders and hams without touching the bone reads 165°F. Add wood and fuel underneath the two ends of the pig as necessary to maintain the smoke and temperature in the smoker, and push cooler embers toward the center.

5 With the help of another person, grasp the two ends of the pig with heat-resistant gloves and flip it over. It may fall apart a bit, which is fine.

6 Pour the remaining basting liquid all over the pig. Cook it for 3 to 4 hours more, or until the shoulders and hams reach an internal temperature of 180°F.

7 Remove the hog from the grates and let it rest for 1 hour, or until it is cool enough to handle with bare hands.

8 Pick apart the meat using your hands, or separate it into large chunks and chop or pull the meat.

PIEDMONT BARBECUE SANDWICH

Style: PIEDMONT

SERVES 4   This is the way barbecue is served in the Piedmont, or western part of North Carolina: sliced or chopped shoulder with some slaw, dressed with a sweet and tangy tomato-vinegar sauce.

4 white hamburger buns
4 cups sliced or chopped pork from Smoked Picnic Ham (page 77)
¼ cup Tomato-Vinegar Sauce (page 96)
2 cups Barbecue Slaw (page 88)

⭐ *This isn't the time to get fancy with the bread. For once, the cheap, highly processed stuff is exactly what you want—assuming you want to have a sandwich exactly the way a real joint would serve it. The idea is that the bread is just a vehicle to hold everything together and soak up some of the flavor.*

On the heel of each bun, place some pork and top it with some Tomato-Vinegar Sauce. Mound some Barbecue Slaw on top of the pork and sauce and then crown each sandwich with the top of the bun.

HUSHPUPPIES

PREP TIME: 10 MINUTES ★ **COOK TIME: 30 MINUTES**

Style: NORTH CAROLINA

SERVES 6   In North Carolina, a tray of barbecue isn't complete without some hushpuppies. Hushpuppies are basically deep-fried balls of cornmeal dough, and there are myriad variations out there. Sadly, many restaurants have taken to using frozen dough or mixes, but as you'll see, they're actually not too difficult to make from scratch.

4 cups vegetable oil

4½ cups finely ground white cornmeal

1 tablespoon baking powder

1 tablespoon sugar

1 tablespoon kosher salt

3 cups water

⭐ *When deep-frying, add the food to the oil in small batches to keep the oil temperature from dropping too much. If you add too much at once, the food will take longer to fry, absorb more oil, and turn soggy.*

1 In a 3-quart pot, heat the oil to 350°F.

2 In a medium bowl, mix together the cornmeal, baking powder, sugar, salt, and water to make a thick batter.

3 Use two tablespoons to scoop and form the batter into oblongs about 2 inches long, and drop each into the hot oil. Deep-fry the hushpuppies for 3 to 4 minutes, or until they float to the top and turn golden brown. Scoop them out of the oil using a slotted spoon and drain on paper towels.

EASTERN NORTH CAROLINA BARBECUE SANDWICH

★ PREP TIME: 5 MINUTES ★

Style: EASTERN NORTH CAROLINA

SERVES 4 In contrast to the Piedmont style, this sandwich makes use of the whole hog, the slaw is mayonnaise-based, and there's no tomato in the sauce. Make sure to mix up bits and pieces from the whole animal for the full, delicious experience.

4 white hamburger buns

4 cups pulled or finely chopped pork from Eastern North Carolina Smoked Whole Hog (page 79)

¼ cup Vinegar–Red Pepper Sauce (page 97)

2 cups Slaw with Mayonnaise Dressing (page 86)

If you like a good amount of tang in your slaw, some barbecue joints add a healthy dose of mustard to the mayonnaise-based dressing— about 2 parts yellow mustard to 1 part mayonnaise.

On the heel of each bun, place some pork and top it with some Vinegar–Red Pepper Sauce. Mound some Slaw with Mayonnaise Dressing on top of the pork and sauce and then crown each sandwich with the top of the bun.

NORTH CAROLINA BRUNSWICK STEW

SERVES 8 Brunswick stew may have begun as a humble combination of squirrel, old bread, and onions, but by the time it arrived in North Carolina, a few welcome additions had made their way into the dish.

3 bacon slices

2 large yellow or white onions, diced

½ cup (1 stick) unsalted butter

½ cup all-purpose flour

2 pounds boneless skinless chicken thighs, diced

1 (28-ounce) can crushed tomatoes

1 pound Yukon Gold potatoes, scrubbed and diced

2 cups fresh or frozen corn kernels, thawed if frozen

2 cups frozen lima beans, thawed

½ cup sugar

8 cups water

1 tablespoon kosher salt

1 tablespoon freshly ground black pepper

1 teaspoon cayenne pepper

⭐ *When cooking flour and butter together to make a roux, it is important to whisk continuously to keep the flour from burning.*

1 In a large pot, cook the bacon over high heat for 1½ to 2 minutes, or until crisp on one side. Reduce the heat to medium, turn the bacon, and cook the other side for 1 to 2 minutes more. Remove the bacon from the pot and set it aside. Do not drain the rendered fat from the pot.

2 Increase the heat to medium-high, add the onions to the pot, and sauté them for 6 to 7 minutes, or until slightly softened.

3 Add the butter to the onions. Once it melts, add the flour, reduce the heat to low, and whisk continuously all over the pan for 3 to 5 minutes or until the mixture is smooth and light brown.

4 Stir in the chicken, tomatoes, potatoes, corn, lima beans, sugar, and water. Crumble the bacon back into the pot. Season the stew with the salt, black pepper, and cayenne. Bring the liquid to a boil, then reduce the heat to a simmer and cook the stew, stirring occasionally, for 1 to 1¼ hours, or until thickened. Serve immediately.

SLAW WITH MAYONNAISE DRESSING

★ PREP TIME: 15 MINUTES, PLUS 30 MINUTES TO CHILL ★

Style: EASTERN NORTH CAROLINA

SERVES 4 This version of coleslaw will strike many Americans as familiar, and it's also the version that's most popular throughout Eastern North Carolina.

1 tablespoon sugar

2 teaspoons kosher salt

1 tablespoon apple cider vinegar

¼ cup Homemade Mayonnaise (page 219) or store-bought

¼ head red cabbage, cored and thinly sliced

¼ head green cabbage, cored and thinly sliced

1 In a large bowl, whisk the sugar and salt into the vinegar until they dissolve. Add the Homemade Mayonnaise and whisk until it is well incorporated.

2 Add the red and green cabbage and toss until well coated with the dressing.

3 Refrigerate the slaw for at least 30 minutes before serving.

⭐ *If you're out of red cabbage, just double the amount of green cabbage. You can also add one grated carrot and one sliced green onion for more color and crunch.*

BARBECUE SLAW

SERVES 4 In the Piedmont region, folks love their barbecue sauce so much that they even use it as a salad dressing. In this version, we add some ketchup and Carolina hot sauce to amp up the flavors.

¼ cup Tomato-Vinegar Sauce (page 96)

1 tablespoon ketchup

1 teaspoon hot sauce, preferably Texas Pete

Kosher salt

Freshly ground black pepper

¼ head red cabbage, cored and thinly sliced

¼ head green cabbage, cored and
  thinly sliced

1 In a large bowl, whisk together the Tomato-Vinegar Sauce, ketchup, and hot sauce. Season it with salt and pepper.

2 Add the red and green cabbage and toss until well coated with the dressing.

3 Refrigerate the slaw for at least 30 minutes before serving.

⭐ *Despite its name, Texas Pete hot sauce is actually a North Carolina brand, which grew out of a business started by Thad Garner and his family. You can find it in the condiment section of most supermarkets.*

SACRILEGIOUS SLAW

Style: PIEDMONT BORDER

SERVES 8 In the no-man's land between the Piedmont and Eastern North Carolina, restaurants have been known to play it a little fast and loose with slaw. You're likely to find a blend of the two traditions, and even though it makes for some funky-looking dressing, it's hard to deny the delicious results.

¼ cup Tomato-Vinegar Sauce (page 96)

1 tablespoon ketchup

1 tablespoon apple cider vinegar

1 tablespoon sugar

2 teaspoons kosher salt

¼ cup Homemade Mayonnaise (page 219) or store-bought

½ head red cabbage, cored and thinly sliced

½ head green cabbage, cored and thinly sliced

1 In a large bowl, whisk together the Tomato-Vinegar Sauce, ketchup, vinegar, sugar, salt, and Homemade Mayonnaise.

2 Add the red and green cabbage and toss until well coated with the dressing.

3 Refrigerate the slaw for at least 30 minutes before serving.

⭐ *Refrigerating coleslaw before serving helps the flavors meld together. Thirty minutes is the recommended minimum, but the longer, the better.*

PULLED PORK HASH

PREP TIME: 15 MINUTES ★ **COOK TIME: 1 HOUR, 40 MINUTES**

Style: SOUTH CAROLINA

SERVES 8 This hash, a pork- or beef-based gravy served over cooked rice, is a side dish unique to South Carolina. It was originally conceived as a way to use up organ meats from a whole pig, simmered for hours until tender. This modernized version makes use of smoked pork shoulder, which drastically cuts down on cooking time.

3 bacon slices

2 large yellow or white onions, diced

4 cups pulled pork from Smoked Picnic Ham (page 77)

1 pound Yukon Gold potatoes, scrubbed and diced

4 cups water

¼ cup apple cider vinegar

1 tablespoon kosher salt

1 tablespoon freshly ground black pepper

1 tablespoon red pepper flakes

2 teaspoons ground mustard

4 tablespoons unsalted butter, melted

⭐ *If you're feeling a little adventurous, add up to ½ cup chopped chicken livers to the mix.*

1 In a large pot, cook the bacon over high heat for 1½ to 2 minutes, or until crisp on one side. Reduce the heat to medium, turn the bacon, and cook the other side for 1 to 2 minutes more. Remove the bacon from the pot and set it aside. Do not drain the rendered fat from the pot.

2 Increase the heat to medium-high, add the onions to the pot, and sauté them for 6 to 7 minutes, or until slightly softened.

3 Add the bacon, pork, potatoes, water, and vinegar to the pot and bring the liquid to a simmer. Season the mixture with the salt, black pepper, red pepper flakes, and ground mustard.

4 Cook the hash for 1½ hours, stirring frequently toward the end, or until all of the liquid has been absorbed. Break up the potatoes as they soften. Stir in the butter. Serve immediately.

COOKED WHITE RICE

PREP TIME: 5 MINUTES ★ **COOK TIME: 25 MINUTES**

Style: SOUTH CAROLINA

SERVES 4   Historically, the Lowcountry was a fertile rice-growing region, so it's no surprise that rice is the preferred bed of choice for South Carolina's iconic barbecue side dish, Pulled Pork Hash (page 91).

2 cups long-grain white rice
2½ cups water

⭐ *Always rinse rice thoroughly before cooking it. The water should run clear once the rice is rinsed.*

1 In a medium pot, bring the rice and water to a boil over high heat.

2 Reduce the heat to very low, cover the pot with a tight-fitting lid, and simmer the rice for 10 to 15 minutes, or until most of the water is absorbed.

3 Turn off the heat and let the rice sit for 10 minutes, covered. Fluff the rice with a fork and serve.

BARBECUED POTATOES

PREP TIME: 5 MINUTES ★ **COOK TIME: 30 MINUTES**

Style: NORTH CAROLINA

SERVES 4   Barbecued potatoes aren't really barbecued—they just got that name because they're often served with barbecue. They're a simple thing to make and a staple of many barbecue joints throughout North Carolina.

**1¼ pounds red or Yukon Gold
  potatoes, scrubbed
Kosher salt**

⭐ *There's no need to peel the potatoes, but do scrub them thoroughly before boiling them to get rid of any dirt.*

1 In a medium pot, cover the potatoes with cold water by 1 inch, salt the water until it tastes like the sea, and bring the water to a boil.

2 Cook the potatoes for 25 to 30 minutes, or until they are fork tender.

3 Drain the potatoes, let them cool a bit, and serve.

CORNBREAD

SERVES 6 If you're not in the mood for hushpuppies, then you've at least got to have some good cornbread to go with your meal. In North Carolina, your meal isn't complete without some kind of cornmeal-based side.

Cooking spray
1½ cups finely ground white cornmeal
1½ teaspoons baking powder
1 teaspoon kosher salt
1¾ cups milk
1 large egg, beaten

⭐ *An interesting variation to try is to use buttermilk instead of milk, which is also traditional in the South.*

1 Preheat the oven to 375°F.

2 Coat an 8-inch square baking dish or 9-inch cast iron skillet with cooking spray.

3 In a medium bowl, mix together the cornmeal, baking powder, and salt. Stir in the milk, followed by the egg.

4 Transfer the batter to the baking dish or skillet and bake the cornbread for 30 minutes, or until golden brown on top.

TOMATO-VINEGAR SAUCE

★ PREP TIME: 5 MINUTES ★
COOK TIME: 5 MINUTES, PLUS OVERNIGHT TO CHILL

Style: PIEDMONT

MAKES ABOUT 1¾ CUPS   This sauce was created when German immigrants moved to the Piedmont region around the time of World War I. At that time, the usual Vinegar–Red Pepper Sauce (page 97) was still being used throughout the state; they adapted it to suit their tastes with the addition of tomato in the form of ketchup.

2 cups apple cider vinegar
½ cup ketchup
2 tablespoons light brown sugar
1 tablespoon red pepper flakes
2 teaspoons cayenne pepper
1 teaspoon kosher salt

⭐ *When making barbecue sauce, simmering the ingredients together instead of simply stirring them together helps the flavors meld.*

1 In a medium saucepan, combine the vinegar, ketchup, brown sugar, red pepper flakes, cayenne, and salt. Bring the liquid to a simmer over medium heat and cook the sauce for 3 to 5 minutes.

2 Let the sauce cool and refrigerate it overnight before using.

VINEGAR-RED PEPPER SAUCE

★ PREP TIME: 5 MINUTES ★
COOK TIME: 5 MINUTES, PLUS OVERNIGHT TO CHILL

Style: EASTERN NORTH CAROLINA

MAKES ABOUT 1¼ CUPS This sauce is the classic accompaniment to barbecue in Eastern North Carolina. For proponents of Eastern North Carolina barbecue, there is no other.

2 cups apple cider vinegar

1 tablespoon red pepper flakes

2 teaspoons cayenne pepper

1 teaspoon kosher salt

⭐ *Although apple cider vinegar is traditional, in a pinch you can use distilled white vinegar instead.*

1 In a medium saucepan, combine the vinegar, red pepper flakes, cayenne, and salt. Bring the liquid to a simmer over medium heat and cook the sauce for 3 to 5 minutes, or until the salt is dissolved.

2 Let the sauce cool and refrigerate it overnight before using.

MUSTARD BARBECUE SAUCE

★ **PREP TIME: 5 MINUTES** ★
COOK TIME: 5 MINUTES, PLUS OVERNIGHT TO CHILL

Style: SOUTH CAROLINA

MAKES ABOUT 1 CUP   In South Carolina, mustard is the base of choice for barbecue sauce, and it is served with all kinds of smoked pork. Pork and mustard, after all, have always been good friends. This version achieves an ideal balance of tanginess, sweetness, and heat, and the use of whole mustard seeds gives the sauce a nice texture.

¼ cup apple cider vinegar

¼ cup Dijon mustard

¼ cup yellow mustard

3 tablespoons honey

1 tablespoon Worcestershire sauce

1 tablespoon vegetable oil

1 tablespoon yellow mustard seeds

1 tablespoon cayenne pepper

1 teaspoon sweet paprika

1 teaspoon kosher salt

⭐ *If you don't have honey, brown sugar is also a perfectly acceptable, traditional choice of sweetener for this sauce.*

1 In a medium bowl, whisk together the vinegar, Dijon mustard, yellow mustard, honey, and Worcestershire sauce to create the wet mixture. Set it aside.

2 In a medium saucepan, heat the oil over medium heat. Add the mustard seeds and cook them for 3 to 5 minutes, or until they start to pop. Add the cayenne, paprika, and salt and cook for 10 seconds, or until fragrant. Stir in the wet mixture and simmer the sauce for about 1 minute, or until the flavors meld.

3 Let the sauce cool and refrigerate it overnight before using.

BANANA PUDDING

PREP TIME: 5 MINUTES ★ COOK TIME: 10 MINUTES

Style: NORTH CAROLINA

SERVES 8 If a North Carolina barbecue joint offers dessert, it's almost certain banana pudding will be one of the choices. Banana pudding is a much beloved dessert no matter what part of the state you're in, and it's very easy to throw together. Classic versions of the dessert top the custard with meringue, but it's also delicious without it.

1 quart heavy (whipping) cream
1 teaspoon pure vanilla extract
4 large egg yolks
¼ cup sugar
1 (9-ounce) box vanilla wafers
2½ pounds ripe bananas, sliced

⭐ *If you end up scrambling some of the egg yolks, use a strainer to separate them out before pouring the custard over the wafers and bananas.*

1 In a medium pot, bring the heavy cream and vanilla to a simmer.

2 In a medium bowl, whisk together the egg yolks and sugar until the mixture is pale yellow.

3 When the cream simmers, whisk in a small amount to the yolk mixture to temper it. Then, whisk that mixture back into the pot of cream. Cook the custard over medium heat for 4 to 5 minutes, or until the mixture coats the back of a spoon and a streak can be drawn through it. Whisk it constantly, especially around the edge of the pan, to make sure the eggs do not scramble.

4 In a 9-by-13-inch baking dish, alternate layers of the wafers and bananas. Once they are all used, pour the custard on top.

5 Refrigerate and chill the pudding completely before serving.

PEACH COBBLER

PREP TIME: 15 MINUTES ★ COOK TIME: 1 HOUR

Style: NORTH CAROLINA

SERVES 8   Peach cobbler goes back a long way, to the pre–Civil War era, and it remains an iconic dessert in North Carolina. Fresh, ripe peaches are a true summer delight, and a good cobbler is worth turning on the oven for.

4 cups sliced fresh peaches

1 cup sugar, divided

Zest and juice of ½ lemon

1 teaspoon pure vanilla extract

1 teaspoon ground cinnamon

½ cup (1 stick) unsalted butter, melted

1 cup all-purpose flour

1 tablespoon baking powder

⭐ *It's really important to use ripe peaches for this, otherwise the flesh won't release from the pit. To prep the peaches, slice each peach in half all the way around the pit, and twist in opposite directions. The two halves should separate easily. Slice thinly using a sharp knife.*

1 Preheat the oven to 375°F.

2 In a medium pot, combine the peaches, ½ cup of sugar, lemon zest and juice, vanilla, and cinnamon. Cook the peaches over high heat, stirring occasionally, for 10 minutes, or until the peaches soften and the sugar dissolves.

3 Pour the butter into a 9-by-13-inch baking dish.

4 In a medium bowl, mix together the flour, baking powder, and remaining ½ cup of sugar. Pour the mixture evenly over the butter, but do not stir it together.

5 Add the peach mixture on top of the flour mixture and bake the cobbler for 45 to 50 minutes, or until golden brown. Serve warm, at room temperature, or chilled.

TYSON HO

Tyson Ho is the owner of Arrogant Swine in Brooklyn, New York, where he smokes whole hogs the North Carolina way. Learn more at www.arrogantswine.com.

How many hogs do you cook in a week?

In the slow season, about two or three; in the summer, about five or six.

What kind are they?

Chester Whites from North Carolina.

Skin-side up or skin-side down?

Both. We always start skin-side up. It allows the meat on the bottom to get that Maillard reaction. And then we finish by flipping it over and basting it.

What does banking the fire contribute to barbecue?

Banking for North Carolina barbecue means taking wood, burning it down to its most carbonized state, and then cutting off the oxygen flow. The coals continue to burn and cook the hog without the aid of any draft. It's a different process for barbecue than other styles. In Texas-style barbecue, the heat and smoke from the burning wood cooks the meat and you need a good flow of oxygen from one end of the smoker to the other. The Carolina process is the complete opposite.

Any advice for first timers?

Look at your animal and ask, "How is it built?" Some pigs have really big shoulders and really small legs. So you have to adjust your fire accordingly.

Do you have an interesting story about cooking a whole hog?

The first time I tried cooking a pig, I got to my house with three guys and realized we didn't have any idea how to get the 100-pound pig off my truck. So we tried getting a clean garbage can and rolling it in there, but the pig was so heavy it bent the plastic can. The pig dropped a few times, and we had to hose it off, but that made it even more slippery. Finally, we got a blanket and carried it off the field M*A*S*H-style, like a dead body— which it was.

What are your thoughts on the future of barbecue in America?

It's kind of like diners eating Chinese food. Look at Chinese food back in the 1980s. Who knew that now there would be restaurants devoted to regional Chinese food that people care about? Americans want to have Shanghai-style buns and lamb from the Mongolian region. And so I think barbecue is that way right now. "No, I don't want barbecue that is adjusted for my ignorance. I want barbecue that's authentic."

TYSON HO'S CAROLINA CHERRY BOUNCE

★ PREP TIME: 5 MINUTES, PLUS 2 WEEKS TO SOAK THE CHERRIES ★

Style: EASTERN NORTH CAROLINA

SERVES 4 "The official cocktail of the city of Raleigh, North Carolina, is the Cherry Bounce. The libation itself predates the signing of the U.S. Constitution and traditionally involves nothing more than just soaking cherries with sugar in brandy or grain alcohol. Isaac Hunter first served the drink in the North Carolina capital back in 1769 at his popular tavern. My modernized version combines a cherry-soaked bourbon with an Italian digestif and a bittersweet fortified wine; it's a variant of the classic whiskey cocktail, the Boulevardier. It is elegant and, because all the ingredients come in equal parts, impossible to forget." —*Tyson Ho*

FOR THE CHERRY BOURBON
1 (750-milliliter) bottle favorite bourbon such as Maker's Mark, Evan Williams, or Jim Beam
8 ounces dried cherries

FOR THE COCKTAILS
4 ounces cherry bourbon
4 ounces Cynar
4 ounces Punt e Mes
4 dashes cherry bitters
4 orange slices, for garnish

⭐ *This recipe scales amazingly for parties. Because it's equal parts everything, you can premix the drink days in advance in whatever quantity you need.*

TO MAKE THE CHERRY BOURBON
Combine the bourbon and cherries in a nonreactive container. Cover and let the cherries soak for 2 weeks.

TO MAKE THE COCKTAILS
1 Put four rocks glasses in the freezer to chill.

2 Chill your mixing glass or punch bowl by filling it with ice and stirring it around for 30 seconds. Dump out the ice.

3 Combine the cherry bourbon, Cynar, Punt e Mes, and cherry bitters in the mixing glass. Fill the mixing glass with ice and stir for 15 seconds.

4 Strain the mixture into the chilled rocks glasses and top off with ice.

5 Garnish each glass with an orange slice and some of the bourbon-soaked dried cherries.

KANSAS CITY

The Kansas City style of barbecue has spread far and wide and is the one most Americans are familiar with even if they don't know it by name. It is imitated widely by barbecue chains and franchises and is the style that dominates the barbecue sauce section of the condiments aisle in most supermarkets. For many people who have seen only a glimpse of barbecue, chances are it was cooked and served in the Kansas City style.

PROTEINS

There is something for everyone in the Kansas City style, so it lends itself to restaurateurs who want to offer a wide range of choices on a menu. In Kansas City, restaurants serve spareribs, baby back ribs, pulled pork, turkey, chicken, beef ribs, brisket, and, of course, the famous burnt ends.

Burnt ends are a Kansas City specialty. They are taken from the end of a cooked brisket, specifically from the end of the point, which is the triangular portion that sits on top of the flat, the other (and larger) half of the brisket. Burnt ends are prized for their rich, particularly smoky flavor, and they make their way into sandwiches and chili.

FLAVORS, RUBS, AND SAUCES

In Kansas City, pitmasters carefully select different types of wood to pair with the meat they are smoking, which greatly influences the flavor. For beef, oak is a popular choice. For pork, there's no question that hickory is the traditional pairing, although apple and cherry are popular second choices for folks looking for a gentler smoke flavor. And for chicken and turkey, which have a more delicate flavor than the other two meats, pecan is a good way to go. Its flavor is similar to hickory, but subtler.

Kansas City–style sauce is sweet and ketchup-based, with just the right amount of vinegar for a bit of tang, and a good amount of brown sugar. Heinz and Kraft brands make the most popular commercially bottled sauces to this day, and they are in the Kansas City style.

FILL THE PLATE

Kansas City isn't just a melting pot when it comes to proteins. The same is true for side dishes that restaurants serve. There are the usual suspects, of course, such as slaw, baked beans, and potato salad. And then there's a nod to Southern cooking with dishes like Dirty Rice (page 119), Old-Fashioned Grits (page 126), and Red Beans and Rice (page 128). In other words, there's plenty to choose from.

POPULAR PAIRINGS

Low-alcohol beers that are "sessionable," meaning ones that allow you to consume a few bottles while still observing moderation, are a popular beverage choice. Pilsners and lagers that offer a crisp contrast to the rich flavors of barbecue are a good way to go.

POINTS TO REMEMBER

★ **Brining or marinating? Use a nonreactive container.** Look for food-grade plastic containers specifically designed for the purpose of brining and marinating, or glass containers. Avoid using aluminum, which can react with acidic ingredients.

★ **Ribs are done when they're done.** With so many bones, it can be difficult to accurately gauge the internal temperature of ribs. Unlike with other cuts of meat, the only way to tell if ribs are done is by look and feel. Ribs are done when you can pull them apart easily with a gentle tug. They should not, however, "fall off the bone," contrary to popular belief.

★ **Use the right wood.** To bring out the flavor of Kansas City barbecue in your meat, seek out hickory, apple, or cherry for pork; oak for beef; and pecan for poultry.

★ **Be on point.** After putting in all the hard work of smoking a brisket, it's important to slice it correctly. Always slice against the grain. The grain on the point (where you get the burnt ends) runs perpendicular to the grain on the flat (the larger, rectangular portion of the brisket underneath the point), so make a mental note where the two separate. The point begins where the meat starts to slope upward and is separated by a thick line of fat running across the width, which you can feel by hand.

★ **Poultry should be cooked to an internal temperature of 165°F.** Use an instant-read thermometer inserted into the thickest part of the meat without touching the bone to keep a constant read on the internal temperature. Because your protein will continue to cook as it rests once you pull it out of the smoker, you can pull it out about 5 degrees early.

SMOKED SPARERIBS

★ PREP TIME: 1 HOUR ★
COOK TIME: 5 HOURS, PLUS 1 HOUR TO REST

Style: KANSAS CITY

SERVES 6 Spareribs are a nice, easy cut for beginners to work with because they have plenty of marbling, which helps keep them from drying out during the smoking process.

2 (4- to 5-pound) racks pork spareribs
3 tablespoons kosher salt
3 tablespoons freshly ground black pepper
Vegetable oil, for brushing the grates
⅔ cup Kansas City–Style Barbecue Sauce
  (page 127)

⭐ *Contrary to popular belief, the meat should not "fall off the bone" when the ribs are done; this is a sign they are overcooked. If you are concerned they will overcook, wrap them in foil for the last 2 hours of cooking.*

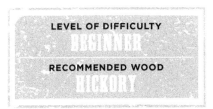

LEVEL OF DIFFICULTY
BEGINNER

RECOMMENDED WOOD
HICKORY

1 Trim the ribs of fat and season them with the salt and pepper (see page 39). Let them stand at room temperature for 1 hour.

2 Preheat the smoker to 225°F to 275°F.

3 If using wood chips or chunks, soak them in water for at least 15 to 30 minutes. Add them to the smoker following the manufacturer's instructions.

4 Oil the smoker grates and place the ribs on them, meat-side up. Close the cooking compartment and smoke the ribs for 3 hours, or until the bark is reddish brown. At this point, you can wrap the ribs in aluminum foil if you are concerned they will lose too much moisture as they finish cooking. Add wood and fuel as necessary to maintain the smoke and temperature in the smoker.

5 Turn over the ribs and continue cooking them for 2 more hours, or until the ribs pull apart with a gentle tug.

6 Remove the foil (if used) and turn the ribs meat-side up again. Baste the racks with the Barbecue Sauce and cook them for 10 more minutes, or until the sauce is set.

7 Remove the ribs from the smoker and let them rest for 1 hour before serving.

SMOKED SPATCHCOCKED CHICKEN

★ **PREP TIME: 1 HOUR, PLUS OVERNIGHT TO BRINE** ★
COOK TIME: 2½ TO 3 HOURS, PLUS 1 HOUR TO REST

Style: **KANSAS CITY**

SERVES 4 TO 6   Brining the chicken keeps it juicy as it cooks, and spatchcocking speeds up the smoking process. Don't forget to remove the giblets from inside the cavity before brining.

1 (4- to 5-pound) chicken
8 cups Master Poultry Brine (page 129)
1 tablespoon kosher salt
3 tablespoons freshly ground black pepper
Vegetable oil, for brushing the grates

⭐ *Avoid cross-contamination when working with chicken by washing your hands with warm water and soap after handling.*

LEVEL OF DIFFICULTY
BEGINNER

RECOMMENDED WOOD
PECAN

1 In a nonreactive container, submerge the chicken in the Master Poultry Brine. Make sure the entire bird is covered by the brine. Refrigerate it overnight.

2 The next day, remove the chicken from the brine and pat it dry. Spatchcock the chicken and season it with the salt and pepper (see page 42). Let it stand at room temperature for 1 hour.

3 Preheat the smoker to 225°F to 250°F.

4 If using wood chips or chunks, soak them in water for at least 15 to 30 minutes. Add them to the smoker following the manufacturer's instructions.

5 Oil the smoker grates and place the chicken on them, skin-side up. Close the cooking compartment and smoke the bird for 2½ to 3 hours, or until an instant-read thermometer inserted without touching the bone reads 160°F. Add wood and fuel as necessary to maintain the smoke and temperature in the smoker.

6 Remove the chicken from the smoker and let it rest for 1 hour. Carve off the breasts, thighs, and legs and serve.

DOC AND SUSAN RICHARDSON

Doc and Susan Richardson are members of the Kansas City Barbeque Society and founders of the Ques Your Daddy BBQ Team. As veterans of the professional circuit, they have won more than 250 awards. Find out more about their team and their restaurant, Doc's Smokehouse, at www.docssmokehouse.com.

***

What would you say you're best known for as pitmasters?

Brisket has always been our strongest category. In 2011, we finished 14th in the country in brisket out of more than 5,000 pro-circuit teams.

Tell us about your history as pitmasters. What were your greatest moments or career highlights?

We've been working the pits for about 30 years, and moved into competition barbecue in 2006. We took Grand Champion in our very first cook, and we were hooked from there!

What are your thoughts on wrapping?

We find it to be extremely useful in tenderizing and expediting cook times. However, we do cook our competition ribs hot and fast, without wrapping. (But that's another story.)

Could you please tell us a little bit about your setup?

We have a large Southern Pride smoker and two Ole Hickory pits. We use a mixture of hickory and cherry woods to achieve our unique flavors and color.

In what ways has the competitive circuit influenced the food at your restaurant?

We want to be Grand Champion cooks every day at the restaurant. As judges, we know the difference between good and great barbecue. Due to cost factors, it's impossible to serve a competition product every time. Most individuals could not afford it. Despite that challenge, our end result is still at the top of the barbecue ladder.

 We use a mixture of hickory and cherry woods to achieve our unique flavors and color.

"QUES YOUR DADDY" SPARERIBS

★ PREP TIME: 1 HOUR ★
COOK TIME: 3 TO 4 HOURS, PLUS 1 HOUR TO REST

Style: KANSAS CITY

SERVES 6 "We use a St. Louis–cut sparerib because good marbling, like a steak, is what you are looking for. Remember: Fat is flavor!" —*Doc and Susan Richardson*

FOR THE BASIC DRY RUB

1 cup brown sugar

1 cup turbinado sugar

3 tablespoons Hungarian or smoked paprika

2 tablespoons ground mustard

2 tablespoons kosher salt

1½ tablespoons granulated garlic

1 tablespoon granulated onion

1 tablespoon ground black pepper

1½ teaspoons cayenne pepper

FOR THE RIBS

2 (4- to 5-pound) racks St. Louis–cut pork spareribs

Vegetable oil, for brushing the ribs and grates

½ cup Basic Dry Rub

1 cup apple juice

1 cup water

Your favorite barbecue sauce (optional)

LEVEL OF DIFFICULTY
BEGINNER

RECOMMENDED WOOD
HICKORY

TO MAKE THE BASIC DRY RUB

In a small bowl, mix the brown sugar, turbinado sugar, paprika, ground mustard, salt, granulated garlic, granulated onion, black pepper, and cayenne. Store in an airtight container until ready to use.

TO MAKE THE RIBS

1 To remove the membrane from the back side of each rack, start on the narrow end of the bone and use a butter knife to lift the edge of the membrane. Grip the edge using a paper towel and pull to remove the membrane completely.

2 Rub oil on both sides of each rack, just enough to moisten them. Season the ribs liberally on both sides with the Basic Dry Rub (although lighter on the back side). Let the ribs sit at room temperature for 1 hour. Add any remaining rub to the ribs right before they go into the smoker.

3 Preheat the smoker to 275°F.

4 If using wood chips or chunks, soak them in water for at least 15 to 30 minutes. Add them to the smoker following the manufacturer's instructions.

➼ "QUES YOUR DADDY" SPARERIBS

5 Oil the smoker grates and place the ribs on them, meat-side up. Close the cooking compartment and cook undisturbed for 2½ hours. Add wood and fuel as necessary to maintain the smoke and temperature in the smoker.

6 In a spray bottle, combine the apple juice and water. At the 2½-hour mark, spray the ribs thoroughly. Continue to cook the ribs and spray them again after 15 minutes.

7 After another 15 minutes (at the 3-hour mark), use a pair of tongs to lift each rack from its center and look at how it bends—if it looks like it's going to break in half, it's done. If not, continue cooking and spraying them, checking every 15 to 20 minutes until they are finished.

8 Glaze the finished ribs with the sauce (if using) on the meat side, and cook for 10 minutes more.

9 Remove the ribs from the smoker and let them rest for 1 hour before serving.

⭐ *For your dry rub, try a bit of an unexpected spice—cinnamon, coriander, thyme, adobo—or just add more or less of the spices above to your taste. Be sure to write down each change you make, and have fun with it.*

BARBECUED BABY BACK RIBS

★ PREP TIME: 1 HOUR ★
COOK TIME: 3 HOURS, PLUS 1 HOUR TO REST

Style: KANSAS CITY

SERVES 4 Baby back ribs are a leaner cut than spareribs and a bit trickier to cook. Just remember to keep the temperature steady inside the cooking chamber and they'll turn out great.

4 (2- to 2½-pound) racks baby back ribs
3 tablespoons kosher salt
3 tablespoons freshly ground black pepper
Vegetable oil, for brushing the grates
⅔ cup Kansas City–Style Barbecue Sauce
   (page 127)

⭐ *The back of pork ribs is covered with a membrane. If you leave it on, it can help keep the ribs from falling apart when you move them. But some pitmasters say it can also prevent the meat from absorbing smoke. Try it both ways to see which you prefer.*

LEVEL OF DIFFICULTY
INTERMEDIATE

RECOMMENDED WOOD
HICKORY

1 Trim the fat from the ribs and season them with the salt and pepper (see page 39). Let them stand at room temperature for 1 hour.

2 Preheat the smoker to 225°F to 275°F.

3 If using wood chips or chunks, soak them in water for at least 15 to 30 minutes and add them to the smoker following the manufacturer's instructions.

4 Oil the smoker grates and place the ribs on them, meat-side up. Close the cooking compartment and cook the ribs for 1½ hours, or until the bark is reddish brown. At this point, you can wrap the ribs in aluminum foil if you are concerned they will lose too much moisture as they continue cooking. Add wood and fuel as necessary to maintain the smoke and temperature in the smoker.

5 Turn over the ribs and continue cooking them for 1½ more hours, or until they pull apart with a gentle tug.

6 Remove the foil (if used) and turn the ribs meat-side up again. Baste the ribs with the Kansas City–Style Barbecue Sauce and cook them for 10 more minutes, or until the sauce is set.

7 Remove the ribs from the smoker and let them rest for 1 hour before serving.

SMOKED SPATCHCOCKED TURKEY

★ **PREP TIME: 1 HOUR, PLUS OVERNIGHT TO BRINE** ★
COOK TIME: 4 TO 4½ HOURS, PLUS 1 HOUR TO REST

Style: KANSAS CITY

SERVES 12   After trying this recipe, you won't want to cook your Thanksgiving turkey any other way. In fact, I bet you won't even wait until Thanksgiving to cook turkey.

1 (12- to 14-pound) whole turkey
6 quarts Master Poultry Brine (page 129)
¼ cup kosher salt
½ cup freshly ground black pepper
Vegetable oil, for brushing the grates

⭐ *When checking the internal temperature of turkey, check the thighs, which take a bit longer to cook than the breasts.*

LEVEL OF DIFFICULTY
INTERMEDIATE
RECOMMENDED WOOD
PECAN

1 In a nonreactive container, submerge the turkey in the Master Poultry Brine, making sure the entire bird is covered by the brine. Refrigerate it overnight.

2 Remove the turkey from the brine and pat it dry. Spatchcock the turkey (see page 43) and season it with the salt and pepper (see page 43). Let it stand at room temperature for 1 hour.

3 Preheat the smoker to 225°F to 275°F.

4 If using wood chips or chunks, soak them in water for at least 15 to 30 minutes. Add them to the smoker following the manufacturer's instructions.

5 Oil the smoker grates and place the turkey flat on them, skin-side up. Close the cooking compartment and smoke the bird for 4 to 4½ hours, or until an instant-read thermometer inserted without touching the bone reads 160°F. Add wood and fuel as necessary to maintain the smoke and temperature in the smoker.

6 Remove the turkey from the smoker and let it rest for 1 hour. Carve off the breasts, thighs, and legs and serve.

BURNT ENDS

★ **PREP TIME: 15 MINUTES** ★
COOK TIME: 3 TO 4 HOURS, PLUS 30 MINUTES TO REST

Style: KANSAS CITY

SERVES 4 Burnt ends are a Kansas City specialty. Every restaurant does them a little differently. Some take the ends from all around the brisket, chop them, and put them back into the smoker to char; some just use the flat; and the best places carve off the point and stick it back into the smoker, then chop it to serve. This recipe follows that tradition. After all, if you're going to cook brisket even longer, it only makes sense to put the fattiest portion back in the smoker.

1 Smoked Beef Brisket (page 172)
Vegetable oil, for brushing the grates

⭐ *At this point, the meat will have already taken on a lot of smoke, so you may want to use a bit less wood than usual or the smoke flavor may be overpowering for some tastes.*

LEVEL OF DIFFICULTY
INTERMEDIATE
RECOMMENDED WOOD
PECAN

1 Separate the point from the flat. The point is the triangular, fattier portion, which sits on top of the flat. You should see a seam of fat running between the two portions. Using a sharp knife, separate the two parts here.

2 Preheat the smoker to 250°F to 275°F.

3 If using wood chips or chunks, soak them in water for at least 15 to 30 minutes. Add them to the smoker following the manufacturer's instructions.

4 Oil the smoker grates and place the point on them, fat-side up. Close the cooking compartment and smoke the point for 3 to 4 hours, or until the exterior is charred. Add wood and fuel as necessary to maintain the smoke and temperature in the smoker.

5 Remove the point from the smoker and wrap it in aluminum foil. Let it rest for 30 minutes to 1 hour. To serve, cut across the grain into ¼-inch-thick slices, or chop into ¾-inch cubes.

BURNT ENDS CHILI

PREP TIME: 5 MINUTES ★ COOK TIME: 1¼ HOURS

Style: KANSAS CITY

SERVES 8 The burnt ends chili at Woodyard BBQ in Kansas City is what put the restaurant on the map, earning it a spot on *Food & Wine* magazine's "Best Chili in the U.S." list. This recipe is inspired by that dish.

1 tablespoon cumin seeds

3 tablespoons vegetable oil

1 yellow onion, chopped

Kosher salt

1 tablespoon tomato paste

1 teaspoon ground ancho chile

1 teaspoon ground chipotle chile

1 teaspoon ground guajillo chile

1 (28-ounce) can diced tomatoes, undrained

2 (15-ounce) cans kidney beans, undrained

4 cups chopped beef from Burnt Ends
    (page 117)

1 In a large pot, heat the cumin seeds in the oil over medium heat for 3 to 4 minutes, or until they are fragrant. Increase the heat to medium-high and add the onion. Sauté the onion for 6 to 7 minutes, or until slightly softened.

2 Season the onion with salt. Stir in the tomato paste and cook for 1 to 2 minutes. Then add the ground chiles, tomatoes with their juices, kidney beans and their liquid, and Burnt Ends to the pot. Bring everything to a simmer and cook for 1 hour, or until thickened. Serve immediately.

★ *If you can't find all the different ground chiles, use 1 tablespoon cayenne pepper instead.*

DIRTY RICE

Style: KANSAS CITY

SERVES 8   Finally, a recipe that makes use of all those chicken livers you've been saving when cooking whole chickens—you have been saving them, right? (Just say yes.) Chicken livers are the secret ingredient to traditional dirty rice, a dish that hails all the way from Louisiana but, luckily for folks in Kansas City, has made its way up the Mississippi.

1 pound smoked sausage, such as andouille, removed from its casing and crumbled

8 ounces chicken livers

2 tablespoons unsalted butter

2 cups finely diced red onion

1 cup finely diced celery

1 cup finely diced green bell pepper

6 garlic cloves, chopped

3 cups Cooked White Rice (page 92)

1¼ cups low-sodium chicken broth

1 tablespoon sweet or smoked paprika

1 tablespoon kosher salt

2 teaspoons cayenne pepper

1 teaspoon freshly ground black pepper

1 teaspoon dried oregano

½ teaspoon ground cinnamon

⭐ *Inside a chicken, you'll typically find the livers in a small bag together with other pieces of offal. The livers are the largest, darkest pieces, are moist and soft to the touch, and smell slightly metallic, like iron. Freeze the livers in a tightly sealed container until you are ready to use them.*

1 In a sauté pan or skillet, cook the sausage and chicken livers over high heat for 7 to 8 minutes, or until browned. Remove them with a slotted spoon and set aside. Once the chicken livers are cool enough to handle, finely chop them.

2 Reduce the heat to medium-high. To the pan, add the butter, onion, celery, bell pepper, and garlic. Sauté, stirring occasionally so the garlic doesn't burn, for 6 to 7 minutes, or until the vegetables are slightly softened.

3 Add the Cooked White Rice and chicken broth to the pan, return the meat to the pan, and season everything with the paprika, salt, cayenne, black pepper, oregano, and cinnamon.

4 Bring the liquid to a simmer and cook, stirring frequently, for 4 to 6 minutes, or until the liquid and seasonings are absorbed. Serve immediately.

KANSAS CITY-STYLE BAKED BEANS

★ PREP TIME: 5 MINUTES, PLUS OVERNIGHT TO SOAK ★
COOK TIME: 2 HOURS

Style: KANSAS CITY

SERVES 8   These baked beans are made the way they're meant to be. They don't start out of a can, and they get plenty of time to cook and develop layers of flavor.

2½ cups dried navy beans

3 bacon slices

1 tablespoon tomato paste

½ cup canned diced tomatoes, drained

3 cups low-sodium beef broth

¼ cup unsulphured blackstrap molasses

2 tablespoons yellow mustard

¼ cup light brown sugar

2 tablespoons kosher salt

⭐ *For an interesting variation, substitute a ham hock for the bacon. Brown it in the beginning before adding the remaining ingredients to the pot, and leave it in to simmer in the oven. Ham hock lends great depth of flavor and body to baked beans.*

1 Put the beans in a large bowl, cover with water, and set aside at room temperature to soak overnight.

2 Drain the beans and place them in a large ovenproof pot. Cover the beans with fresh water by 2 inches. Bring the water to a boil, reduce the heat to a simmer, and cook the beans for 30 to 35 minutes, or until tender. Drain.

3 Preheat the oven to 350°F.

4 Wipe out the pot, and cook the bacon over high heat for 1½ to 2 minutes, or until crisp on one side. Reduce the heat to medium, turn the bacon, and cook the other side for 1 to 2 minutes more. Remove the bacon from the pot and set aside. Do not drain the rendered fat from the pot.

5 Reduce the heat to low, add the tomato paste, and cook for 1 minute. Return the beans to the pot, along with the diced tomatoes, beef broth, molasses, mustard, sugar, and salt. Crumble the bacon into the pot, cover the pot, and transfer it to the oven. Bake for 70 to 80 minutes, or until the baked beans have thickened. Serve immediately.

EASTERN EUROPEAN POTATO SALAD

PREP TIME: 10 MINUTES ★ **COOK TIME: 15 MINUTES**

Style: KANSAS CITY

SERVES 4 In the early twentieth century, Kansas City was a magnet for Eastern European immigrants, many of whom got into the meatpacking trade. It was a major hub of cattle operations, thanks to its position on the railways leading to Chicago. These immigrants brought with them their food traditions, contributing to the melting pot of barbecue in the region.

1¼ pounds baby red and white potatoes, scrubbed

½ teaspoon kosher salt, plus more for the boiling water

⅓ cup extra-virgin olive oil

3 tablespoons apple cider vinegar

1 teaspoon caraway seeds

3 celery stalks, including leaves, finely chopped

¼ cup diced red onion

⭐ *Toasting caraway seeds intensifies their flavor. Place them in a skillet in a single layer over low heat and toast briefly, just until they are fragrant and steam rises.*

1 Put the potatoes in a medium pot, cover with cold water by 1 inch, and salt the water until it tastes like the sea. Bring the water to a boil and cook the potatoes for 13 to 15 minutes, or until fork tender.

2 While the potatoes are cooking, in a medium bowl, whisk together the olive oil, vinegar, caraway seeds, and ½ teaspoon of salt. Set aside.

3 Drain the potatoes, let them cool, and cut them into halves or quarters, depending on their size. Transfer to the bowl with the dressing and toss to coat.

4 Add the chopped celery and onion and toss until everything is well coated. Serve immediately.

CORNSLAW

Style: KANSAS CITY

SERVES 6 For those looking for a slight twist on the usual cabbage-based slaw, corn makes an interesting and pleasantly sweet addition in the summer months, when fresh corn is abundant and at its peak.

4 teaspoons sugar

2½ teaspoons kosher salt

4 teaspoons apple cider vinegar

⅓ cup Homemade Mayonnaise (page 219) or store-bought

¼ head red cabbage, cored and thinly sliced

¼ head green cabbage, cored and thinly sliced

2 cups fresh or frozen corn kernels, thawed if frozen

1 In a large bowl, whisk the sugar and salt into the vinegar until they dissolve. Add the Homemade Mayonnaise and whisk until incorporated.

2 Add the red and green cabbage and corn and toss until well coated with the dressing.

3 Refrigerate the cornslaw for 30 minutes before serving.

⭐ *When buying fresh corn, choose ears with bright green, tightly closed husks. The silk should be moist and not brown.*

HOMEMADE FRENCH FRIES

PREP TIME: 20 MINUTES ★ **COOK TIME: 30 MINUTES**

Style: KANSAS CITY

SERVES 4   French fries are a popular side at many barbecue joints throughout Kansas City, and cooking them up from scratch makes all the difference in flavor and texture.

4 cups vegetable oil
2 pounds russet potatoes
Kosher salt
Freshly ground black pepper

⭐ *Frying the potatoes twice gives them a fluffy interior and a crisp, golden exterior, and keeps them from turning soggy. Blanching in the oil at the lower temperature cooks the inside of the potatoes and frying at the higher temperature finishes the outside.*

1 In a 3-quart pot, heat the oil to 300°F.

2 Peel and cut the potatoes into matchstick-size pieces. Put them in a bowl of cold water.

3 When ready to fry, squeeze the potatoes dry by placing them in a kitchen towel and wringing them out.

4 Add the potatoes to the oil and blanch them, in batches to prevent overcrowding, until they float to the top and the bubbles subside (they should not brown), 4 to 5 minutes; drain the fries on paper towels.

5 When all the potatoes have been blanched, increase the oil temperature to 400°F.

6 Fry, in batches again, until crisp and golden, 1 to 2 minutes. Drain the fries on paper towels and immediately season them with salt and pepper.

OLD-FASHIONED GRITS

PREP TIME: 10 MINUTES ★ **COOK TIME: 1 HOUR**

Style: KANSAS CITY

SERVES 6   Grits may be a staple of the South, but Kansas City is a melting pot of peoples where traditions from all over the country meet, so it's no surprise that it will pop up every once in a while in restaurants in the region.

6 cups water

1 tablespoon kosher salt

1 cup white grits, preferably stone-ground

1 cup milk

4 tablespoons unsalted butter

1 teaspoon freshly ground black pepper

⭐ *Stone-ground grits from the higher-end brands, such as Anson Mills, can take a bit longer to cook. This is because their grains are less uniform, so while most of your batch will be cooked, there will still be some hard larger pieces. Just keep cooking until those larger pieces soften. Don't worry: Your grits won't overcook.*

1 In a large pot, bring the water and salt to a boil over high heat. Add the grits in a steady stream while whisking constantly.

2 Reduce the heat to medium-low and cook the grits for at least 45 minutes, or until thickened and tender. Start whisking them again when they start to thicken, whisking more frequently as it approaches the hour mark.

3 Stir in the milk and butter and season with the pepper. Cook for 15 more minutes, or until the butter and milk are fully incorporated. Serve hot.

KANSAS CITY-STYLE BARBECUE SAUCE

★ PREP TIME: 5 MINUTES ★
COOK TIME: 3 MINUTES, PLUS OVERNIGHT TO CHILL

Style: KANSAS CITY

MAKES ABOUT 1½ CUPS   This ketchup- and brown sugar–based sauce is typical of the Kansas City style of barbecue. It's a crowd pleaser: Well balanced and mild, it goes with just about anything.

1 cup ketchup

½ cup apple cider vinegar

2 tablespoons Worcestershire sauce

2 tablespoons unsulphured blackstrap molasses

6 tablespoons light brown sugar

2 tablespoons vegetable oil

6 garlic cloves, finely chopped

2 teaspoons kosher salt

2 teaspoons sweet paprika

1 teaspoon ground cinnamon

1 teaspoon cayenne pepper

⭐ *When making barbecue sauce, it's not necessary to boil the ingredients, only simmer them. Simmering allows the flavors to meld; boiling causes the ingredients to separate.*

1 In a medium bowl, whisk together the ketchup, vinegar, Worcestershire sauce, molasses, and brown sugar to create the wet mixture. Set aside.

2 In a medium saucepan, heat the oil over medium heat. Add the garlic and cook for about 30 seconds, or until golden. Stir in the salt, paprika, cinnamon, and cayenne and cook for 10 seconds, or until fragrant.

3 Add the wet mixture to the pan, stir, and simmer everything for about 1 minute, or until the flavors meld.

4 Let the sauce cool and refrigerate it overnight before using.

RED BEANS AND RICE

PREP TIME: 15 MINUTES ★ **COOK TIME: 15 MINUTES**

Style: KANSAS CITY

SERVES 6   Here's another Southern tradition that Kansas City has borrowed from its friends down the Mississippi.

2 tablespoons unsalted butter

1 cup finely diced red onion

5 garlic cloves, finely chopped

3 cups Cooked White Rice (page 92)

1 (15-ounce) can kidney beans, undrained

1 cup low-sodium chicken broth

1 tablespoon cayenne pepper

1 tablespoon sweet or smoked paprika

1 teaspoon dried oregano

1 teaspoon dried thyme

1 teaspoon kosher salt

1 teaspoon freshly ground black pepper

1 In a medium pot, heat the butter over medium-high heat. Add the onion and garlic and sauté, stirring occasionally so the garlic doesn't burn, for 6 to 7 minutes, or until slightly softened.

2 Add the Cooked White Rice, kidney beans and their liquid, and chicken broth to the pot; season with the cayenne, paprika, oregano, thyme, salt, and black pepper. Bring the liquid to a simmer and cook until the liquid and seasonings are absorbed, 4 to 6 minutes. Serve immediately.

★ *Store spices in a cool, dry place away from light. Whole spices generally last longer than ground spices; stored properly, whole spices have a shelf life of up to a year, while ground spices start to lose their potency after about six months.*

MASTER POULTRY BRINE

PREP TIME: 1 MINUTE ★ **COOK TIME: 10 MINUTES**

Style: KANSAS CITY

MAKES ABOUT 2 CUPS Chicken is one of the four categories of meat officially judged at contests sanctioned by the Kansas City Barbeque Society. Most participants brine their chicken before smoking it. Here's a competition-worthy brine that you may like to try.

2 garlic cloves, crushed

5 fresh thyme sprigs

2 tablespoons kosher salt

1 tablespoon black peppercorns

1 tablespoon white peppercorns

1 teaspoon coriander seeds

1 teaspoon cane sugar

2 cups water

1 In a medium saucepan, combine the garlic, thyme, salt, black and white peppercorns, coriander seeds, sugar, and water. Bring the liquid to a boil to dissolve the sugar and salt.

2 Let the brine cool. Transfer it to an airtight container and refrigerate it until completely chilled before using.

⭐ *When brining, it's important to use a nonreactive container such as glass or food-grade plastic.*

MEM

MEMPHIS

emphis, like Kansas City, flourished after the Civil War thanks to its location and local industry. While Kansas City made its fortunes on beef, Memphis drew its strength from lumber. (Is it just a coincidence that these two industries give you the ingredients for barbecue?) ★ And like Kansas City, the town grew rapidly, attracting African American residents from points farther south who were looking for economic opportunities. With them, they brought their barbecue traditions and influenced the Memphis barbecue scene. ★ Unlike Kansas City, however, Memphis became a party town. The city's infamous nightlife was fueled by music, and many of the city's first barbecue restaurants popped up along Beale Street, where late-night crowds would spill out of bars and nightclubs looking for something satisfying to eat. Mighty Memphis barbecue certainly fit the bill.

PROTEINS

Memphis is a pork town, but it's rare to see restaurants cook the whole hog. Instead, they specialize in shoulders or ribs. When it comes to shoulders, most restaurants opt for just part of it—either the butt or the picnic. Everyone has their reasons, of course, for preferring one or the other, but in the end, it all culminates in an amazing variety of dishes that are unique to Memphis, like Barbecue Nachos (page 151), which are the de facto snack at a Redbirds game, and Barbecue Spaghetti (page 152), which is a staple at two Memphis institutions, Jim Neely's Interstate Bar-B-Que and the Bar-B-Q Shop.

You can get ribs two different ways: wet or dry. Wet ribs are basted with barbecue sauce just before they come out of the smoker, or right after, while dry ribs are not a reference to badly cooked ribs, but rather a dry rub that is unique to Memphis. The original dry ribs were created by Charlie Vergos at a place called the Rendezvous. Vergos doesn't like to call them "dry ribs," preferring the name "Rendezvous ribs," but it's what everyone else seems to call them. Whatever you call them, they're delicious, and while he won't divulge the rub recipe to anyone, you can taste dried oregano, a nod to his Greek heritage.

No discussion of smoked meat in Memphis would be complete without mentioning Barbecued Bologna (page 141). It's exactly what it sounds like: a big hunk of bologna smoked for a few hours until a nice crust forms around the outside. It's served sliced or cubed, and sometimes it's deep-fried before being served.

Last, but not least, you'll see the occasional Cornish game hen, also a Memphis specialty. The Cozy Corner has been doing them for a very long time, and their spicy rub is downright addictive. You'll find a recipe for game hen in this chapter, and while it won't be the same as going there, it is definitely a juicy, tasty bird.

FLAVORS, RUBS, AND SAUCES

When it comes to pork, the only seasoning that many pitmasters use is hickory smoke. No salt and no pepper. Those are the absolute purists. Others, though, will slather mustard all over their shoulders or ribs before seasoning with salt and pepper, which helps the seasoning stick without altering the final flavor. Poultry seasoning gets a bit more creative, incorporating ingredients like paprika, garlic powder, onion powder, oregano, and sugar.

Most Memphis restaurants offer two versions of a molasses- and ketchup-based sauce: mild and hot. Some places make it really hot; even locals can be surprised at the level of heat. The hot version in this chapter doesn't turn it up to 11, but it does leave a pleasant tingle in the back of the throat.

FILL THE PLATE

Memphians don't get terribly distracted by sides. There's slaw, and an interesting version of baked beans that uses the "outside brown" of a pork shoulder, which is the tasty, crispy bits of bark on the outside.

POPULAR PAIRINGS

Iced tea and cold beer are the way to go in Memphis. Popular local breweries include Wiseacre Brewing and Ghost River Brewing.

POINTS TO REMEMBER

★ **Be a soft touch.** A slather, like mustard, helps seasoning stick to the surface of meat, but lay it on too thick, and it can clump up and hinder smoke absorption. Use just enough to lightly coat the surface.

★ **Wrap ribs.** While pork shoulder has plenty of fat to keep it moist as it cooks, ribs are a little tricky for beginners. If it's your first time smoking ribs, consider wrapping them in aluminum foil during the cooking process to keep them juicy.

★ **Move with care.** Avoid using tongs to pick up cooked ribs. Instead, put on barbecue gloves and pick them up by hand.

★ **Create your own rub.** Making up a rub is a great way to get started on creating your own signature style. As a rule of thumb, about half of it should consist of salt, as the main purpose of a rub is to draw moisture to the surface of the meat to attract smoke.

★ **Storing barbecue.** The best way to store leftover barbecue is to portion it out into vacuum-seal bags and keep them in the refrigerator. To reheat, simply drop the bags into boiling water.

DRY-RUBBED SPARERIBS

★ **PREP TIME: 1 HOUR** ★
COOK TIME: 5 HOURS, PLUS 1 HOUR TO REST

Style: MEMPHIS

SERVES 6   Charlie Vergos, proprietor of the Rendezvous in Memphis, is the origina-tor of the dry rub rib style that Memphis is famous for. He calls them "Rendezvous ribs." And he's careful not to say that they're barbecue, either; his are cooked hot and fast over a charcoal fire. This version is smoked low and slow but uses a rub inspired by his ribs.

2 (4- to 5-pound) racks pork spareribs
¼ cup yellow or Dijon mustard
6 tablespoons Memphis Rib Rub (page 161)
Vegetable oil, for brushing the grates

⭐ *Mustard is the slather of choice in Memphis. Apply it in a thin layer uniformly all over the meat to help the rub stick.*

LEVEL OF DIFFICULTY
BEGINNER

RECOMMENDED WOOD
HICKORY

1 Trim the fat from the ribs, slather them with the mustard, and season all over with the Memphis Rib Rub (see page 161). Let them stand at room temperature for 1 hour.

2 Preheat the smoker to 225°F to 275°F.

3 If using wood chips or chunks, soak them in water for at least 15 to 30 minutes. Add them to the smoker following the manu-facturer's instructions.

4 Oil the smoker grates and place the ribs on them, meat-side up. Close the cooking compartment and cook the ribs for 3 hours, or until the bark is reddish brown. At this point, you may choose to wrap the ribs in aluminum foil if you are concerned they will lose too much moisture as they continue to cook. Add wood and fuel as necessary to maintain the smoke and temperature in the smoker.

5 Turn over the ribs and continue cooking for 2 more hours, or until the ribs pull apart with a gentle tug.

6 Remove the ribs from the smoker, discard the foil (if used), and let them rest for 1 hour before serving.

CLINT CANTWELL

Clint Cantwell is the pitmaster of the Smoke in da Eye barbecue team and editor of Kingsford.com and Grillocracy .com (aka "The People's Republic of Smoke and Flame"). In May 2015, he was named one of the "Ten Faces of Memphis Barbecue" by *Memphis* magazine.

What's the deal with smoked bologna?

According to Mark Lambert of Sweet Swine O'Mine championship barbecue team, this dish more than likely has roots in gas stations, as a quick on-the-go meal. Bologna could be kept warm, then sliced or cubed and thrown into the deep fryer, and served with cheese and crackers. Today, entire chubs of bologna are scored, thrown in the smoker, then sliced and served on sandwiches.

How does competition-level barbecue differ from restaurant barbecue?

The food cooked for the judges at contests is rarely what you'd serve in your backyard or in a restaurant setting. With competition barbecue, the goal is to create the perfect bite for the judges, so teams tend to use injections to enhance flavor and moisture.

What's behind the trend of restaurants switching to gas-fired cookers?

The key to a successful barbecue joint is the ability to ensure that customers experience the same high quality every time, and that often means using non-wood-fired smokers. There is something special about a restaurant that is only open as long as the meat on the smoker lasts, like Franklin Barbecue in Austin, but that's not necessarily practical for a large restaurant with a full staff and set hours of operation.

What are your thoughts on wrapping?

Wrapping is something that you see across the country and especially in the competition world. There are definitely purists who shun the practice, but cooks should do what works best for them, and often that means wrapping brisket, pork butt, or ribs for a portion of the cooking time to ensure tenderness.

 With competition barbecue, the goal is to create the perfect bite for the judges...

CLINT CANTWELL'S MEMPHIS DRY-RUBBED WINGS

PREP TIME: 15 MINUTES ★ **COOK TIME: 2 HOURS**

Style: MEMPHIS

SERVES 6   "In a nod to Memphis's famed dry-rubbed ribs, this recipe features chicken wings that have been seasoned and then smoked to perfection. They're so good, in fact, that you won't miss the sauce at all!" —*Clint Cantwell*

¼ cup smoked paprika

3 tablespoons brown sugar

1½ tablespoons kosher salt

1 tablespoon onion powder

1 tablespoon granulated garlic

2 teaspoons ground mustard

1½ teaspoons freshly ground black pepper

1 teaspoon dried oregano

1 teaspoon dried thyme

1 teaspoon ground cumin

24 chicken wings

Vegetable oil, for brushing the grates

⭐ *Smoking the wings at a higher temperature than normal allows the skin to crisp up nicely. Since the cooking time is so short (as far as barbecue goes, at least) you don't have to worry about them drying out.*

1 In a medium bowl, mix together the paprika, brown sugar, salt, onion powder, granulated garlic, ground mustard, pepper, oregano, thyme, and cumin. Season the chicken wings well with the dry rub mixture.

2 Preheat the smoker to 300°F.

3 If using wood chips or chunks, soak them in water for at least 15 to 30 minutes. Add them to the smoker following the manufacturer's instructions.

4 Oil the smoker grates and place the wings on them. Close the cooking compartment and smoke the wings for 2 hours, or until an instant-read thermometer inserted without touching the bone reads 165°F. Add wood and fuel as necessary to maintain the smoke and temperature in the smoker. Serve immediately.

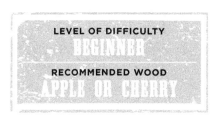

LEVEL OF DIFFICULTY
BEGINNER

RECOMMENDED WOOD
APPLE OR CHERRY

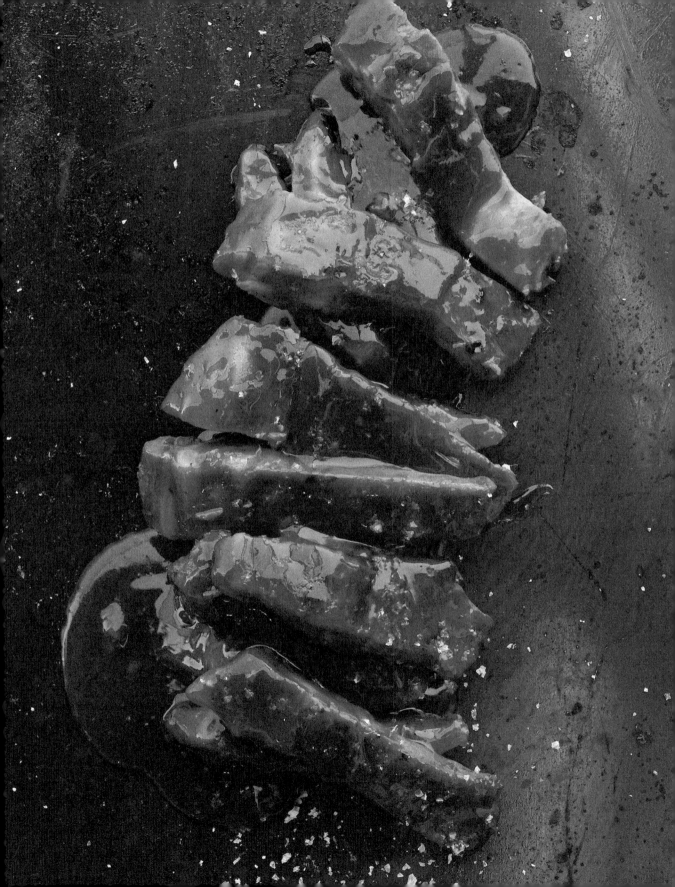

MEMPHIS-STYLE WET SPARERIBS

★ **PREP TIME: 1 HOUR** ★
COOK TIME: 5 HOURS, PLUS 1 HOUR TO REST

Style: MEMPHIS

SERVES 6 This recipe is similar to the Dry-Rubbed Spareribs (page 135), except that a layer of barbecue sauce is slathered on at the end of the cooking process. Or, you can do like they do at Corky's BBQ in Memphis and make what they call a half-and-half: Cover half of the ribs with dry rub and the other half with sauce.

2 (4- to 5-pound) racks pork spareribs
¼ cup yellow or Dijon mustard
3 tablespoons kosher salt
3 tablespoons freshly ground black pepper
Vegetable oil, for brushing the grates
⅔ cup Mild Memphis-Style Barbecue Sauce (page 159)

⭐ *If you buy St. Louis–cut spareribs, you can skip all the trimming and just start cooking right away. They're a little more expensive, but sometimes paying for convenience is worth it.*

LEVEL OF DIFFICULTY
BEGINNER

RECOMMENDED WOOD
HICKORY

1 Trim the fat from the ribs, slather them with the mustard, and season all over with the salt and pepper (see page 39). Let them stand at room temperature for 1 hour.

2 Preheat the smoker to 225°F to 275°F.

3 If using wood chips or chunks, soak them in water for at least 15 to 30 minutes. Add them to the smoker following the manufacturer's instructions.

4 Oil the smoker grates and place the ribs on them, meat-side up. Close the cooking compartment and cook the ribs for 3 hours, or until the bark is reddish brown. At this point, you may choose to wrap the ribs in aluminum foil if you are concerned they will lose too much moisture as they continue to cook. Add wood and fuel as necessary to maintain the smoke and temperature in the smoker.

➡➡

➤ MEMPHIS-STYLE WET SPARERIBS

5 Turn over the ribs and continue cooking them for 2 more hours, or until the ribs pull apart with a gentle tug.

6 Remove the ribs from the smoker and discard the foil (if used). Baste them with the Mild Memphis-Style Barbecue Sauce, return them to the smoker, and cook them meat-side up for 10 minutes more, or until the sauce is set.

7 Remove the ribs from the smoker and let them rest for 1 hour before serving.

BARBECUED BOLOGNA

★ **PREP TIME: 1 HOUR** ★
COOK TIME: 4 HOURS, PLUS 1 HOUR TO REST

Style: MEMPHIS

SERVES 6   Barbecued bologna is a common local delicacy in Memphis. For those who haven't had it before, we'll answer the question that's likely on your mind right now in the affirmative: Yes, it is bologna as in the lunch meat. And it's typically served with white bread.

1 (3- to 4-pound) piece beef bologna
2 tablespoons yellow or Dijon mustard
1 tablespoon kosher salt
1 tablespoon freshly ground black pepper
Vegetable oil, for brushing the grates

⭐ *Scoring the bologna helps the smoke penetrate the interior.*

LEVEL OF DIFFICULTY
BEGINNER

RECOMMENDED WOOD
HICKORY

1 Make ¼-inch-deep cuts all over the bologna, 1 inch apart.

2 Slather the bologna all over with the mustard and season it with the salt and pepper. Let it stand at room temperature for 1 hour.

3 Preheat the smoker to 225°F to 275°F.

4 If using wood chips or chunks, soak them in water for at least 15 to 30 minutes. Add them to the smoker following the manufacturer's instructions.

5 Oil the smoker grates and place the bologna on them. Close the cooking compartment and smoke the bologna for 4 hours, or until a nice crust has formed around the outside. Add wood and fuel as necessary to maintain the smoke and temperature in the smoker.

6 Remove the bologna from the smoker and let it rest for 1 hour. Slice and serve.

BARBECUED BOLOGNA SANDWICH

PREP TIME: 5 MINUTES ★ **COOK TIME: 5 MINUTES**

Style: MEMPHIS

SERVES 4   While barbecued bologna is delicious just the way it is for a quick snack, for a more substantial meal, folks turn to this decadent treat.

4 cups vegetable oil

4 (½-inch-thick) slices Barbecued Bologna (page 141)

1 cup Mild Memphis-Style Barbecue Sauce (page 159)

4 white hamburger buns

2 cups Sweet 'n' Tangy Slaw (page 155)

⭐ *The pot you use to deep-fry should be filled only about one-third of the way with oil. This allows room for the oil to expand when food is added.*

1 In a 3-quart pot, heat the oil to 350°F.

2 Fry each bologna slice, one at a time, for 1 minute. Remove it from the oil using tongs and drain the slices on paper towels.

3 In a medium bowl, toss the bologna with the Barbecue Sauce until thoroughly coated.

4 On the heel of each bun, place a bologna slice. Top each slice with a mound of Sweet 'n' Tangy Slaw and crown the sandwich with the top of the bun.

DRY-RUBBED BABY BACK RIBS

★ **PREP TIME: 1 HOUR** ★
COOK TIME: 3 HOURS, PLUS 1 HOUR TO REST

Style: MEMPHIS

SERVES 4 Baby back ribs are the universal crowd pleaser. They're lean, tender, and meaty and, when seasoned just right, they don't need any sauce at all.

4 (2- to 2½-pound) racks baby back ribs
¼ cup yellow or Dijon mustard
6 tablespoons Memphis Rib Rub (page 161)
Vegetable oil, for brushing the grates

 *A full rack of baby back ribs should contain 11 to 13 bones.*

LEVEL OF DIFFICULTY
INTERMEDIATE
RECOMMENDED WOOD
HICKORY

1 Trim the fat from the ribs, slather them with the mustard, and season all over with the Memphis Rib Rub (see page 161). Let them stand at room temperature for 1 hour.

2 Preheat the smoker to 225°F to 275°F.

3 If using wood chips or chunks, soak them in water for at least 15 to 30 minutes. Add them to the smoker following the manufacturer's instructions.

4 Oil the smoker grates and place the ribs on them, meat-side up. Close the cooking compartment and cook the ribs for 1½ hours, or until the bark is reddish brown. At this point you may choose to wrap the ribs in aluminum foil if you are concerned they will lose too much moisture as they continue to cook. Add wood and fuel as necessary to maintain the smoke and temperature in the smoker.

5 Turn over the ribs and continue cooking them for 1½ hours more, or until the ribs pull apart with a gentle tug.

6 Remove the ribs from the smoker, discard the foil (if used), and let them rest for 1 hour before serving.

MEMPHIS-STYLE WET BABY BACK RIBS

★ **PREP TIME: 1 HOUR** ★
COOK TIME: 3 HOURS, PLUS 1 HOUR TO REST

Style: MEMPHIS

SERVES 4   The tomato- and molasses-based barbecue sauce that is popular throughout Memphis gives baby back ribs incomparable depth of flavor.

4 (2- to 2½-pound) racks baby back ribs
3 tablespoons kosher salt
3 tablespoons freshly ground black pepper
Vegetable oil, for brushing the grates
⅔ cup Mild Memphis-Style Barbecue Sauce (page 159)

⭐ *When your ribs are ready to take off the grill, put on insulated gloves and use your hands to move them instead of a pair of tongs. Tongs can tear through the bark that's formed on the exterior.*

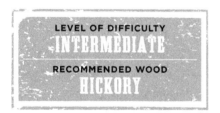

LEVEL OF DIFFICULTY
INTERMEDIATE
RECOMMENDED WOOD
HICKORY

1 Trim the fat from the ribs and season them with the salt and pepper (see page 39). Let them stand at room temperature for 1 hour.

2 Preheat the smoker to 225°F to 275°F.

3 If using wood chips or chunks, soak them in water for at least 15 to 30 minutes. Add them to the smoker following the manufacturer's instructions.

4 Oil the smoker grates and place the ribs on them, meat-side up. Close the cooking compartment and cook the ribs for 1½ hours, or until the bark is reddish brown. At this point you can wrap the ribs in aluminum foil if you are concerned they will lose too much moisture as they cook. Add wood and fuel as necessary to maintain the smoke and temperature in the smoker.

5 Flip the ribs and cook for 1½ hours more, or until they are easily pulled apart.

6 Remove the ribs from the smoker and discard the foil (if used). Baste the ribs with the Mild Memphis-Style Barbecue Sauce. Return the ribs to the smoker and cook them meat-side up for 10 more minutes, or until the sauce is set.

7 Remove the ribs from the smoker and let them rest for 1 hour before serving.

SMOKED CORNISH GAME HENS

★ PREP TIME: 1 HOUR ★
COOK TIME: 1½ HOURS, PLUS 30 MINUTES TO REST

Style: MEMPHIS

SERVES 4 Fruitwood is a great match for the delicate flavor of these small birds. Cornish game hens may seem like an odd thing to smoke, especially since they take only an hour to cook, but they're a local favorite: Cozy Corner (as far as we know) is the only place in Memphis that does them, and they do them right, if the loyal clientele is any indication.

4 (1¼-pound) Cornish game hens
¼ cup yellow or Dijon mustard
2 tablespoons kosher salt
2 tablespoons freshly ground black pepper
2 teaspoons sweet paprika
2 teaspoons cayenne pepper
Vegetable oil, for brushing the grates

⭐ *Despite the short cooking time, the skin on the hens should crisp up nicely.*

LEVEL OF DIFFICULTY
INTERMEDIATE
RECOMMENDED WOOD
APPLE OR CHERRY

1 Slather the hens with the mustard. In a small bowl, combine the salt, black pepper, paprika, and cayenne. Season the hens with the mixture. Let them stand at room temperature for 1 hour.

2 Preheat the smoker to 275°F to 285°F.

3 If using wood chips or chunks, soak them in water for at least 15 to 30 minutes. Add them to the smoker following the manufacturer's instructions.

4 Oil the smoker grates and place the hens on them, skin-side up. Close the cooking compartment and smoke the birds for 1 to 1½ hours, or until an instant-read thermometer inserted without touching the bone reads 160°F. Add wood and fuel as necessary to maintain the smoke and temperature in the smoker.

5 Remove the hens from the smoker and let them rest for 30 minutes before serving.

CLINT CANTWELL'S CHILI-LIME SPATCHCOCKED CHICKEN

★ PREP TIME: 10 MINUTES, PLUS 4 HOURS TO BRINE ★
COOK TIME: 1½ HOURS

Style: MEMPHIS

SERVES 4 "Smoked chicken has rarely tasted better than it does in this recipe for whole chili-lime rubbed butterflied (spatchcocked) chicken. By removing the backbone from the chicken and smoking it bone-side down, you are not only allowing the chicken to slow roast without drying out or burning from direct flame but also making sure the dark and white meat cook evenly." —*Clint Cantwell*

FOR THE CHILI-LIME SALT

2 tablespoons kosher salt

1½ teaspoons brown sugar

1 teaspoon grated lime zest

1 teaspoon chili powder

FOR THE CHICKEN

8 cups water

¼ cup kosher salt

¼ cup brown sugar

1 (3-pound) chicken

¼ cup olive oil

Vegetable oil, for brushing the grates

⭐ *Coating chicken or turkey skin with oil and smoking it at a higher temperature than usual can help it crisp up nicely.*

LEVEL OF DIFFICULTY
INTERMEDIATE

RECOMMENDED WOOD
PECAN

TO MAKE THE CHILI-LIME SALT

In a small bowl, stir together the salt, brown sugar, lime zest, and chili powder. Store in an airtight container until ready to use.

TO MAKE THE CHICKEN

1 In a nonreactive container large enough to hold the chicken, combine the water, salt, and brown sugar; stir until the salt has completely dissolved.

2 Spatchcock the chicken (see page 43) and submerge it in the brine. Be sure the chicken is completely covered by the brine. Refrigerate the chicken for 4 to 6 hours.

3 Remove the chicken from the brine, rinse it, and pat dry. Coat both sides of the chicken with the olive oil, then season it liberally with the chili-lime salt.

4 Preheat the smoker to 325°F.

5 If using wood chips or chunks, soak them in water for at least 15 to 30 minutes. Add them to the smoker following the manufacturer's instructions.

6 Oil the smoker grates and place the chicken on them, bone-side down. Close the cooking compartment and smoke the chicken for 1½ hours, or until an instant-read thermometer inserted without touching the bone reads 160°F.

7 Remove the chicken from the smoker and let it rest for 1 hour before slicing and serving.

HICKORY-SMOKED BOSTON BUTT

★ **PREP TIME: 30 MINUTES** ★
COOK TIME: 9½ TO 10½ HOURS, PLUS 1 HOUR TO REST

Style: MEMPHIS

SERVES 12   In Memphis, many restaurants have shifted from cooking whole shoulders to cooking just butts, or the upper part of the shoulder. They cook faster and yield more meat per pound.

1 (7- to 8-pound) bone-in Boston butt
2 tablespoons yellow or Dijon mustard
3 tablespoons kosher salt
3 tablespoons freshly ground black pepper
Vegetable oil, for brushing the grates

⭐ *For longer smoke jobs, try a combination of wood chips and chunks. Chips provide a lot of initial smoke, while chunks go through a slow burn to keep a steady level of smoke going later on.*

LEVEL OF DIFFICULTY
INTERMEDIATE
RECOMMENDED WOOD
HICKORY

1 Trim the fat from the butt, slather it with the mustard, and season it with the salt and pepper (see page 39). Let it stand at room temperature for 1 hour.

2 Preheat the smoker to 275°F to 285°F.

3 If using wood chips or chunks, soak them in water for at least 15 to 30 minutes. Add them to the smoker following the manufacturer's instructions.

4 Oil the smoker grates and place the butt on them. Close the cooking compartment and cook the butt for 7 to 7½ hours, or until an instant-read thermometer inserted without touching the bone reads 165°F. At this point you may choose to wrap the butt in aluminum foil if you are concerned it will lose too much moisture as it continues to cook. Add wood and fuel as necessary to maintain the smoke and temperature in the smoker.

5 Turn over the butt and continue cooking it for 2½ to 3 hours more, or until the internal temperature reaches 190°F.

6 Remove the butt from the smoker, discard the foil (if used), and let it rest for 1 hour. Discard the bones and pull or chop the meat. Mix in the crispy exterior with the meat when serving.

MEMPHIS-STYLE PULLED PORK SANDWICH

★ **PREP TIME: 5 MINUTES** ★

Style: MEMPHIS

SERVES 4   In Memphis, this sandwich is synonymous with barbecue. In fact, when ordering, hardly anyone asks for a sandwich. Instead, they ask for "a barbecue."

4 cups pulled or finely chopped pork from Hickory-Smoked Boston Butt (page 148)
1 cup Mild Memphis-Style Barbecue Sauce (page 159)
4 white hamburger buns
2 cups Sweet 'n' Tangy Slaw (page 155)

1 In a medium bowl, toss the pork with the Mild Memphis–Style Barbecue Sauce until thoroughly coated.

2 On the heel of each bun, place some pork. Add a mound of Sweet 'n' Tangy Slaw on top of the pork and then crown each sandwich with the top of the bun.

⭐ *Make sure each sandwich gets a bit of the exterior bark, or "outside brown," for the best eating experience.*

BARBECUE NACHOS

PREP TIME: 10 MINUTES ★ **COOK TIME: 10 MINUTES**

Style: MEMPHIS

SERVES 4 If you ever get the chance to go to a ballgame in Memphis, you'll see most of the crowd chowing down on a basket of delicious barbecue nachos, which are topped with—what else?—pulled pork.

3 cups pulled pork from Hickory-Smoked Boston Butt (page 148)

⅓ cup Mild Memphis-Style Barbecue Sauce (page 159)

4 cups tortilla chips

1 cup shredded Monterey Jack cheese

1 jalapeño, sliced thinly

⅓ cup diced white onion

1 (15-ounce) can black beans, rinsed and drained

1 Preheat the oven to 350°F.

2 In a medium bowl, toss the pork with the Mild Memphis–Style Barbecue Sauce until thoroughly coated.

3 In a 9-by-13-inch baking dish, scatter the tortilla chips roughly in a single layer. Distribute the pulled pork, cheese, jalapeño slices, onion, and black beans over the chips.

4 Bake the nachos for 5 to 10 minutes, or just until the cheese melts.

⭐ *When making nachos, look for nice, thick tortilla chips that can stand up to the weight of the toppings.*

BARBECUE SPAGHETTI

PREP TIME: 15 MINUTES ★ COOK TIME: 15 MINUTES

Style: MEMPHIS

SERVES 8   Brady Vincent is credited with the invention of this dish. Vincent was the owner of Brady and Lil's, a landmark restaurant that became one of Memphis's first African American–owned barbecue joints to attract a white clientele in the 1960s. This recipe is an attempt to recreate his iconic dish.

Kosher salt

1 pound spaghetti

2 tablespoons unsalted butter

1 yellow onion, chopped

1 green bell pepper, seeded, stemmed, and chopped

2 cups Mild Memphis-Style Barbecue Sauce (page 159)

4 cups pulled pork from Hickory-Smoked Boston Butt (page 148)

½ cup chopped fresh basil

½ cup chopped fresh flat-leaf parsley

★   *Although most pasta recipes call for noodles to be cooked al dente, or with a bit of bite left, in Memphis the spaghetti is cooked until soft for this dish.*

1 Bring a large pot of salted water to a boil over high heat. Add the spaghetti and cook until it is soft, 11 to 13 minutes. Drain the pasta and set aside.

2 Meanwhile, in a large skillet, melt the butter over medium-high heat. Add the onion and bell pepper and sauté for 6 to 7 minutes, or until slightly softened. Season the vegetables with salt.

3 Add the Mild Memphis–Style Barbecue Sauce to the skillet and bring it to a simmer. Stir in the spaghetti and pulled pork and cook for 1 to 2 minutes, or until heated through. Stir in the basil and parsley. Serve immediately.

BARBECUE STEW

PREP TIME: 5 MINUTES ★ **COOK TIME: 40 MINUTES**

Style: MEMPHIS

SERVES 10 TO 12   Cook barbecue often enough, and you'll start to notice one thing: It tends to make for a lot of leftovers. In a way, it's a bit like figuring out what to do after Thanksgiving. Well, here's a Memphis treat that might just become a go-to recipe.

2 tablespoons unsalted butter

1 large white or yellow onion, diced

1 (28-ounce) can crushed tomatoes

4 cups pulled pork

4 cups diced red or white potatoes

1 pound okra, stemmed and cut into
    ½-inch rounds

1 cup fresh or frozen corn kernels, thawed
    if frozen

1 (15-ounce) can pinto beans, rinsed
    and drained

2 cups low-sodium chicken broth

1 tablespoon kosher salt

1 tablespoon freshly ground black pepper

1 tablespoon sweet paprika

1 tablespoon dried oregano

1 teaspoon cayenne pepper

1 In a large pot, melt the butter over medium-high heat. Add the onion and sauté for 6 to 7 minutes, or until slightly softened. Add the tomatoes, pork, potatoes, okra, corn, pinto beans, and chicken broth. Season everything with the salt, black pepper, paprika, oregano, and cayenne.

2 Bring the liquid to a boil. Reduce the heat to a simmer and cook the stew, stirring occasionally, for 20 to 25 minutes, or until it is thickened and the flavors meld. Serve immediately.

⭐ *Using low-sodium chicken broth allows you to exercise greater control over the amount of salt in your dish.*

BARBECUE PIZZA

PREP TIME: 5 MINUTES ★ COOK TIME: 10 MINUTES

Style: MEMPHIS

SERVES 1 TO 2   The barbecue pizza originated at an Italian restaurant called Coletta's in the 1950s. It proved popular with military folks returning from the war who had been stationed in Italy, and apparently it was also a favorite of Elvis Presley's, who used to ask his wife to pick up several boxes to take back to his home in Graceland. This version is gussied up a bit from the original, which is just a regular cheese pizza with barbecue. But we think Gouda and red onion are a nice combination with barbecue sauce and pork.

1 (12-inch) pre-baked pizza crust

1 tablespoon Mild Memphis-Style Barbecue Sauce (page 159)

2 cups shredded Gouda cheese

1 cup pulled pork from Hickory-Smoked Boston Butt (page 148)

¼ cup thinly sliced red onion

1 Preheat the oven to 450°F.

2 Brush the pizza crust with the Barbecue Sauce. Scatter the cheese, pork, and onion all over the top.

3 Place the pizza on a baking sheet and bake for 8 to 10 minutes, or until the crust is golden brown.

⭐ *Depending on your oven and how many toppings are on the crust, pre-made pizza crust might take a little longer to cook than the package directions state. If it's still not done by the stated time, bake for another 5 minutes.*

SWEET 'N' TANGY SLAW

Style: MEMPHIS

SERVES 4   While some Memphis barbecue joints lean toward the super tangy when it comes to their slaw—putting a good dose of mustard and vinegar in the dressing—and others go creamy and sweet, most strike a balance somewhere in the middle. This one strikes that balance.

2 tablespoons sugar

2 teaspoons kosher salt

2 tablespoons apple cider vinegar

2 tablespoons yellow mustard

¼ cup Homemade Mayonnaise (page 219) or store-bought

¼ head red cabbage, cored and thinly sliced

¼ head green cabbage, cored and thinly sliced

1 In a large bowl, whisk the sugar and salt into the vinegar until they dissolve. Add the Homemade Mayonnaise and whisk until incorporated.

2 Add the red and green cabbage and toss until well coated.

3 Refrigerate the slaw for at least 30 minutes before serving.

⭐ *To store any unused portion of cabbage, wrap it tightly in plastic wrap and refrigerate for up to 1 week.*

CLINT CANTWELL'S GRILLED SOUTHERN COLESLAW

PREP TIME: 10 MINUTES ★ COOK TIME: 20 MINUTES

Style: MEMPHIS

SERVES 8 TO 10 "Impress your guests this grilling season with a twist on traditional coleslaw featuring grilled cabbage, charred red pepper, pickled ginger, and a tangy Southern dressing." —*Clint Cantwell*

1 cup Homemade Mayonnaise (page 219) or store-bought

¼ cup apple cider vinegar

2 teaspoons sugar

½ teaspoon kosher salt

¼ teaspoon freshly ground black pepper

1 head cabbage, cut into eighths with the core intact

Cooking spray

1 red bell pepper

2 tablespoons minced pickled ginger

⭐ *When grilling vegetables, avoid moving them around on the grill as they cook or the char marks won't appear.*

1 In a small bowl, mix together the Homemade Mayonnaise, vinegar, sugar, salt, and pepper. Refrigerate the dressing until you are ready to use it.

2 Prepare a grill for medium-high heat cooking, about 400°F.

3 Spray both sides of each cabbage section with the cooking spray. Place each section over direct heat and grill the cabbage for about 5 minutes per side, or until char marks are visible. Remove the cabbage from the grill and immediately refrigerate it or place it in a cooler on ice to stop the cooking process.

4 Place the red bell pepper on the grill and char the skin on all sides, 8 to 10 minutes total. Remove it from the grill. Once it is cool enough to handle, remove the stem and core, and cut it into thin strips.

5 Finely chop the cooled cabbage and place it in a large bowl, along with the charred bell pepper strips, pickled ginger, and dressing. Toss everything to coat with the dressing. Refrigerate the slaw until ready to serve.

BARK 'N' BEANS

★ PREP TIME: 5 MINUTES, PLUS OVERNIGHT TO SOAK ★
COOK TIME: 2 HOURS

Style: MEMPHIS

SERVES 8　This variation on baked beans uses the bark, or "outside brown," from a pulled pork shoulder to give the dish an incredibly deep, meaty flavor.

2½ cups dried navy beans

1 tablespoon vegetable oil

1 tablespoon tomato paste

1 cup "outside brown" from Hickory-Smoked Boston Butt (page 148)

½ cup canned diced tomatoes, drained

3 cups low-sodium beef broth

½ cup unsulphured blackstrap molasses

¼ cup yellow mustard

2 tablespoons kosher salt

⭐ *Before soaking dried beans, spread them out in a single layer on a baking sheet or similar surface and scan for any rocks or other debris. It's rare, but sometimes these things end up in the mix.*

1 Put the beans in a large bowl, cover with water, and set aside at room temperature to soak overnight.

2 Drain the beans, place them in a large ovenproof pot, and cover them with fresh water by 2 inches. Bring the water to a boil, reduce the heat to a simmer, and cook the beans for 30 to 35 minutes, or until tender. Drain.

3 Preheat the oven to 350°F.

4 In a large ovenproof pot, heat the vegetable oil over low heat. Add the tomato paste and cook it for 1 minute. Add the beans, outside brown, diced tomatoes, beef broth, molasses, mustard, and salt to the pot and stir everything to combine.

5 Cover the pot and transfer it to the oven. Bake the beans for 70 to 80 minutes, or until thickened.

MILD MEMPHIS-STYLE BARBECUE SAUCE

★ PREP TIME: 5 MINUTES ★
COOK TIME: 3 MINUTES, PLUS OVERNIGHT TO CHILL

Style: MEMPHIS

MAKES ABOUT 1½ CUPS Tomato and molasses form the base for this easy-to-make barbecue sauce that exemplifies the Memphis style.

¾ cup unsulphured blackstrap molasses

½ cup distilled white vinegar

½ cup ketchup

1 teaspoon kosher salt

1 teaspoon sweet paprika

1 teaspoon garlic powder

½ teaspoon ground cumin

1 In a small pot, combine the molasses, vinegar, ketchup, salt, paprika, garlic powder, and cumin. Bring the sauce to a simmer and cook it for 1 to 2 minutes, or until the flavors meld.

2 Let the sauce cool and refrigerate it overnight before using.

⭐ *Blackstrap molasses is the darkest version of molasses available, which is key to creating the characteristic color and complex flavor of this sauce.*

HOT MEMPHIS-STYLE BARBECUE SAUCE

★ PREP TIME: 5 MINUTES ★
COOK TIME: 5 MINUTES, PLUS OVERNIGHT TO CHILL

Style: MEMPHIS

MAKES ABOUT 1 CUP Memphis barbecue restaurants usually offer two sauces: a mild and a hot. This one packs just the right amount of punch.

1 tablespoon vegetable oil
1 jalapeño, seeded and finely diced
¾ cup unsulphured blackstrap molasses
½ cup distilled white vinegar
½ cup ketchup
1 teaspoon kosher salt
1 teaspoon cayenne pepper
1 teaspoon sweet paprika
½ teaspoon ground cumin
½ teaspoon garlic powder

1 In a small pot, heat the oil over medium heat. Add the jalapeño and cook it for 2 to 3 minutes, or until softened. Stir in the molasses, vinegar, ketchup, salt, cayenne, paprika, cumin, and garlic powder. Bring the sauce to a simmer and cook it for 1 minute, or until the flavors meld.

2 Let the sauce cool and refrigerate it overnight before using.

⭐ *Jalapeños can vary quite a bit in terms of how hot they are. It depends on their ripeness: Riper jalapeños are hotter. You can distinguish the milder from the hotter by looking at the skin, which will start to wrinkle and turn red as it ripens.*

MEMPHIS RIB RUB

Style: MEMPHIS

MAKES ABOUT 1 CUP Many Greek Americans went into the restaurant business in Memphis at the turn of the twentieth century. Their influence is important to the development of the region's barbecue style. One influence is the common use of oregano in dry rub for ribs.

½ cup kosher salt

2 tablespoons freshly ground black pepper

2 tablespoons sweet paprika

2 tablespoons dried oregano

2 teaspoons cayenne pepper

2 teaspoons garlic powder

In a small bowl, thoroughly combine all the ingredients. Store in an airtight container until ready to use.

⭐ *Generally, most stores carry both sweet and smoked paprika, which can come from either Spain or Hungary. (There are more grades in between, but it's rare to find them in the United States.) Sweet paprika is what most recipes mean when they call for just "paprika," while smoked paprika lends a fantastic savory flavor that is definitely worth trying.*

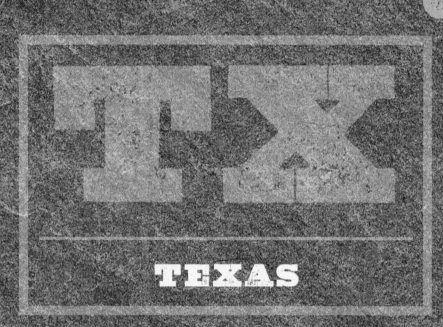

TEXAS

obb Walsh, author of the *Legends of Texas Barbecue Cookbook,* says, "Texas barbecue is a feisty mutt with a whole lot of crazy relatives." In other words, Texas is so big, it's no surprise that it is home to many different barbecue traditions. ★ Texas barbecue can be divided into four regions: Hill Country, Central Texas, South Texas, and East Texas. We'll go over the major differences in the next two sections.

PROTEINS

Although Texas barbecue is often associated with beef, folks in the Lone Star State actually eat plenty of pork, too, and even the occasional turkey, chicken, and goat.

East Texas barbecue was heavily influenced by the cooking traditions of cotton-picking slaves who came from Mississippi and Alabama in the 1850s. There, you'll find spareribs, the occasional rack of baby backs, and "hot links," or spicy beef sausages.

Central Texas is all about brisket, cooked low and slow with indirect smoke from pecan or oak, and also beef sausages prepared in the German-Czech tradition.

In contrast, the Hill Country and South Texas are known for styles that diverge from what purists consider traditional barbecue. In other words, wood smoke is not used to cook the meat, nor is it a major flavoring agent.

In the Hill Country, beef brisket, beef ribs, and the occasional goat are cooked hot and fast, not low and slow, using direct heat from mesquite coals. The juices drip down onto the coals and create some smoke, which is reminiscent of the direct heat method traditional to North Carolina barbecue, but with a bolder wood and hotter fire. It's closer to grilling than smoking.

In South Texas, the Mexican tradition of barbacoa involves wrapping a cow head in *maguey* leaves, which come from the agave plant, and burying it with coals in a pit in the ground. It's more of a family event that is best experienced outside of restaurants, which often resort to steaming beef tongues and cheeks—about as far from barbecue as you can get.

FLAVORS, RUBS, AND SAUCES

When it comes to seasoning and sauces, there's plenty of variation and, contrary to popular belief, the whole of Texas isn't strictly "no sauce" territory. As with proteins, it really depends on the region.

In East Texas, there's plenty of sauce to be had, and the Mississippi influence is apparent—thick and red, it's sweetened with plenty of brown sugar (sometimes to the point where it's a bit grainy) and often flavored with plenty of cumin, too.

Central Texas is probably where Texas barbecue got its no-sauce reputation. Following the traditions brought by German and Czech immigrants who opened meat markets in the region, most Central Texas joints stick to salt and pepper and are more likely to serve some pickles, sliced white onion, and white bread with 'cue than sauce.

Get into Hill Country and sauce is pretty rare, too, but if it does make an appearance, it's thin and vinegar-based, which sounds an awful lot like the stuff served in Eastern North Carolina, but don't tell that to the cowboys.

In South Texas, if you're fortunate enough to encounter real barbacoa, the traditional accompaniment is salsa and tortillas.

FILL THE PLATE

Side dishes throughout Texas are standard fare: coleslaw, potato salad, and baked pinto beans, with the occasional Mexican or German-Czech twist. Some places serve Texas toast, and in Central Texas they really get into pickles.

POPULAR PAIRINGS

An ice-cold pilsner or lager with moderate alcohol content and good drinkability is definitely the way to go with Texas barbecue.

POINTS TO REMEMBER

★ **Trim carefully.** When trimming the fat from a brisket, create a smooth surface along the meat that will allow the smoke to flow freely and eliminate any jagged edges, which will burn.

★ **Start with Prime.** USDA-graded beef comes in three grades: Select, Choice, and Prime. Prime is the highest, and it has the best kind of marbling—fine flecks of fat that look like snow woven throughout the muscle. If you're cooking brisket for the first time, Prime beef will make it easier. Even though it is the most expensive, it also gives you a greater margin of error against drying out the meat.

★ **Make sure it's whole.** Many supermarkets sell only the flat of the brisket these days, so when you shop for brisket, insist on getting a whole packer brisket. You'll see the difference because one end (the point) will slope upward from the rest of the meat.

★ **Don't get shorted on ribs.** When shopping for beef ribs, ask for whole beef short ribs. If the butcher tries to gives you back ribs instead, politely refuse. These come from the part of the animal that also yields prime rib roast or rib steaks. Understandably, butchers want to make the biggest roasts and steaks that they can and usually leave mere scraps on the bones.

★ **Consider wrapping.** If it's your first time making brisket, consider wrapping it in aluminum foil partway through the cooking process to keep it moist. Although some pitmasters affectionately refer to this as the "Texas crutch," it's hard to argue with the consistent result, and many of the country's best pitmasters use this technique.

SMOKED TURKEY BREAST

SERVES 4   Turkey breast may not be the first thing that comes to mind for most people when they think of Texas barbecue, but plenty of barbecue joints serve it and, when done well, it is surprisingly popular. Slice thinly to serve in sandwiches throughout the week, or cube it for a delicious white turkey chili—the possibilities are limitless.

2 (2½- to 3-pound) bone-in turkey
    breast halves
¼ cup Texas Dry Rub (page 189)
Vegetable oil, for brushing the grates

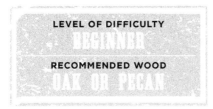 *Avoid turkey breasts that have been "enhanced" with commercial brine or saltwater solutions whenever possible, as these often contain preservatives and chemical additives.*

LEVEL OF DIFFICULTY
BEGINNER

RECOMMENDED WOOD
OAK OR PECAN

1 Pull the skin off the breasts and season them with the Texas Dry Rub (see page 189). Let them stand at room temperature for 1 hour.

2 Preheat the smoker to 225°F to 275°F.

3 If using wood chips or chunks, soak them in water for at least 15 to 30 minutes. Add them to the smoker following the manufacturer's instructions.

4 Oil the smoker grates and place the turkey on them, meat-side up. Close the cooking compartment and cook the breasts for 2½ to 3 hours. At this point, you can choose to wrap the breasts in aluminum foil if you are concerned they will lose too much moisture as they continue to cook. Add wood and fuel as necessary to maintain the smoke and temperature in the smoker.

5 Continue cooking the breasts for 1 hour more, or until an instant-read thermometer inserted without touching the bone reads 160°F.

6 Remove the breasts from the smoker, discard the foil (if used), and let them rest for 30 minutes before serving.

EAST TEXAS SPARERIBS

★ **PREP TIME: 1 HOUR** ★
COOK TIME: 5 HOURS, PLUS 1 HOUR TO REST

Style: EAST TEXAS

SERVES 6   In East Texas, ribs are coated with a thick, tomato-based sauce sweetened with plenty of brown sugar and heavily spiced with cumin.

2 (4- to 5-pound) racks pork spareribs
3 tablespoons kosher salt
3 tablespoons freshly ground black pepper
Vegetable oil, for brushing the grates
⅔ cup East Texas Barbecue Sauce (page 191)

⭐ *When shopping for spareribs, avoid racks that have shiners, or areas of exposed bone. These can ruin your crust as the ribs cook. And you're also paying more for less meat.*

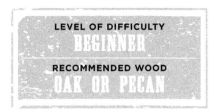

LEVEL OF DIFFICULTY
BEGINNER

RECOMMENDED WOOD
OAK OR PECAN

1 Trim the fat from the ribs and season them with the salt and pepper (see page 39). Let them stand at room temperature for 1 hour.

2 Preheat the smoker to 225°F to 275°F.

3 If using wood chips or chunks, soak them in water for at least 15 to 30 minutes. Add them to the smoker following the manufacturer's instructions.

4 Oil the smoker grates and place the ribs on them, meat-side up. Close the cooking compartment and cook the ribs for 3 hours, or until the bark is reddish brown. At this point you may choose to wrap the ribs in aluminum foil if you are concerned they will lose too much moisture as they continue to cook. Add wood and fuel as necessary to maintain the smoke and temperature in the smoker.

5 Turn over the ribs and continue cooking them for 2 hours more, or until the ribs pull apart with a gentle tug.

6 Remove the ribs from the smoker and discard the foil (if used). Baste the ribs with the East Texas Barbecue Sauce, return them to the smoker, and cook them meat-side up for 10 more minutes, or until the sauce is set.

7 Remove the ribs from the smoker and let them rest for 1 hour before serving.

EAST TEXAS BABY BACK RIBS

★ PREP TIME: 1 HOUR ★

COOK TIME: 3 HOURS, PLUS 1 HOUR TO REST

Style: EAST TEXAS

SERVES 4 If you're after incredibly tender ribs glazed with a thick, sweet sauce, then these baby back ribs are the way to go. Napkins are necessary for cleaning hands and faces after feasting on these.

4 (2- to 2½-pound) racks baby back ribs
3 tablespoons kosher salt
3 tablespoons freshly ground black pepper
Vegetable oil, for brushing the grates
⅔ cup East Texas Barbecue Sauce (page 191)

⭐ *A good rack of ribs should have its fat spread evenly throughout its length.*

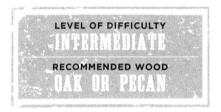

LEVEL OF DIFFICULTY
INTERMEDIATE
RECOMMENDED WOOD
OAK OR PECAN

1 Trim the fat from the ribs and season them with the salt and pepper (see page 39). Let them stand at room temperature for 1 hour.

2 Preheat the smoker to 225°F to 275°F.

3 If using wood chips or chunks, soak them in water for at least 15 to 30 minutes. Add them to the smoker following the manufacturer's instructions.

4 Oil the smoker grates and place the ribs on them, meat-side up. Close the cooking compartment and cook the ribs for 1½ hours, or until the bark is reddish brown. At this point you may choose to wrap the ribs in aluminum foil if you are concerned they will lose too much moisture as they continue to cook. Add wood and fuel as necessary to maintain the smoke and temperature in the smoker.

5 Turn over the ribs and continue cooking them for 1½ hours more, or until they pull apart with a gentle tug.

6 Remove the ribs from the smoker and discard the foil (if used). Baste the ribs with the East Texas Barbecue Sauce, return them to the smoker, and cook them meat-side up for 10 more minutes, or until the sauce is set.

7 Remove the ribs from the smoker and let them rest for 1 hour before serving.

SMOKED BEEF RIBS

★ **PREP TIME: 1 HOUR** ★
COOK TIME: 5 TO 6 HOURS, PLUS 1 HOUR TO REST

Style: CENTRAL TEXAS

SERVES 6   The Central Texas style is all about simple seasoning and taking on great flavor from oak and pecan smoke. That's why these ribs get just a generous coating of salt and pepper before going into the smoker.

1 (3- to 5-pound) rack beef short ribs
2 tablespoons kosher salt
2 tablespoons freshly ground black pepper
Vegetable oil, for brushing the grates

⭐ *Look for ribs from the plate section of the animal, not the chuck. For the very best short ribs, ask your butcher for the sixth, seventh, and eighth bones in one rack.*

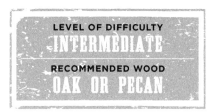

LEVEL OF DIFFICULTY
INTERMEDIATE
RECOMMENDED WOOD
OAK OR PECAN

1 Trim the fat from the ribs and season them with the salt and pepper (see page 41). Let them stand at room temperature for 1 hour.

2 Preheat the smoker to 275°F.

3 If using wood chips or chunks, soak them in water for at least 15 to 30 minutes. Add them to the smoker following the manufacturer's instructions.

4 Oil the smoker grates and place the ribs on them, meat-side up. Close the cooking compartment and smoke the ribs for 5 to 6 hours, or until an instant-read thermometer inserted without touching the bone reads 200°F. Add wood and fuel as necessary to maintain the smoke and temperature in the smoker.

5 Remove the ribs from the smoker and let them rest for 1 hour before serving.

COFFEE-RUBBED SHORT RIBS

★ PREP TIME: 1 HOUR ★
COOK TIME: 5 TO 6 HOURS, PLUS 1 HOUR TO REST

Style: TEXAS

SERVES 6 Looking for a seasoning with a little more oomph than plain old salt and pepper? The deep, earthy notes of coffee pair particularly well with the richness of beef short ribs.

1 (3- to 5-pound) rack beef short ribs
¼ cup Coffee-Chili Dry Rub (page 190)
Vegetable oil, for brushing the grates

⭐ *For an interesting variation, substitute unsweetened cocoa powder for the instant coffee in the dry rub.*

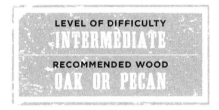

LEVEL OF DIFFICULTY
INTERMEDIATE
RECOMMENDED WOOD
OAK OR PECAN

1 Trim the fat from the ribs and season them with the Coffee-Chili Dry Rub (see page 190). Let them stand at room temperature for 1 hour.

2 Preheat the smoker to 275°F.

3 If using wood chips or chunks, soak them in water for at least 15 to 30 minutes. Add them to the smoker following the manufacturer's instructions.

4 Oil the smoker grates and place the ribs on them, meat-side up. Close the cooking compartment and smoke the ribs for 5 to 6 hours, or until an instant-read thermometer inserted without touching the bone reads 200°F. Add wood and fuel as necessary to maintain the smoke and temperature in the smoker.

5 Remove the ribs from the smoker and let them rest for 1 hour before serving.

SMOKED BEEF BRISKET

★ **PREP TIME: 1 HOUR** ★
COOK TIME: 7½ TO 9½ HOURS, PLUS 1 TO 2 HOURS TO REST

Style: CENTRAL TEXAS

SERVES 6 TO 8   Here it is: the cut that Texas is famous for the world over. Cooking a brisket may seem like a big project, but just remember that the same principles are at work here—seasoning, temperature control, and resting—and you'll be just fine.

1 (8- to 10-pound) brisket
3 tablespoons kosher salt
3 tablespoons freshly ground black pepper
Vegetable oil, for brushing the grates

⭐ *The grain in each part of the brisket—the flat and the point—runs in two different directions. Roughly speaking, the grain in the point runs perpendicular to the grain in the flat, so you'll want to slice the two sections separately.*

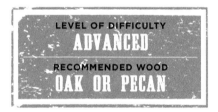

LEVEL OF DIFFICULTY
ADVANCED

RECOMMENDED WOOD
OAK OR PECAN

1 Trim the fat from the brisket and season it with the salt and pepper (see page 41). Let it stand at room temperature for 1 hour.

2 Preheat the smoker to 225°F to 275°F.

3 If using wood chips or chunks, soak them in water for at least 15 to 30 minutes. Add them to the smoker following the manufacturer's instructions.

4 Oil the smoker grates and place the brisket on them, fat-side up. Close the cooking compartment and cook the brisket for 5 to 6 hours, or until the bark is dark brown. At this point, you may choose to wrap the brisket in aluminum foil if you are concerned it will lose too much moisture as it continues to cook. Add wood and fuel as necessary to maintain the smoke and temperature in the smoker.

5 Turn over the brisket and continue cooking it for 2½ to 3½ hours more, or until the internal temperature reaches 200°F.

6 Remove the brisket from the smoker, discard the foil (if used), and let it rest for 1 to 2 hours. To serve, cut the meat against the grain into ¼-inch-thick slices.

NOT-YOUR-AVERAGE BRISKET SANDWICH

★ **PREP TIME: 5 MINUTES** ★

Style: EAST TEXAS

SERVES 4   While folks in Texas are often sticklers for tradition when it comes to barbecue, the sandwich is the one medium that leaves room for a little creativity. (Heck, you're already going to be slathering your brisket in some sauce, anyway.) This brisket sandwich gets a pleasant tang from pickled red onions and an interesting kick thanks to a topping of chipotle slaw.

4 cups chopped meat from Smoked Beef
   Brisket (page 172)
1 cup East Texas Barbecue Sauce (page 191)
4 white hamburger buns
2 cups Chipotle Slaw (page 184)
½ cup Pickled Red Onion (page 178)

⭐ *Save sliced brisket in vacuum-seal bags; for the best flavor, reheat the meat by placing the bags directly in simmering water.*

1 In a medium bowl, toss the brisket with the East Texas Barbecue Sauce until thoroughly coated.

2 On the heel of each bun, place some brisket. Top each with some Chipotle Slaw and Pickled Red Onion and then crown each sandwich with the top of the bun.

BBQ PULLED CHICKEN SANDWICH

★ PREP TIME: 15 MINUTES ★

Style: TEXAS

SERVES 4 Okay, so even in Texas, every once in a while, folks will 'fess up to craving a chicken sandwich. Hey, it happens. Well, just like with anything else related to barbecue in the Lone Star State, nobody jokes around with this. But because it is a chicken sandwich, there's a little room for creativity. So we borrowed some spatchcocked chicken from over the border (shh, don't tell Kansas City), a bit of sauce from the East, and German-Czech slaw from the heart of Texas to make a crazy good chicken sandwich.

1 quart pulled chicken from Smoked
   Spatchcocked Chicken (page 111)
1 cup East Texas Barbecue Sauce (page 191)
4 sesame buns
½ cup Pickled Red Onion (page 178)
1½ cups Central Texas Coleslaw (page 185)

1 In a medium bowl, toss the chicken with the East Texas Barbecue Sauce until thoroughly coated.

2 On the heel of each bun, place the chicken. Top with the Pickled Red Onion, Central Texas Coleslaw, and the crown of the bun.

⭐ *Pulling chicken is easy. Break it up into large chunks, and then pull it apart with your hands or use two forks to shred it. Aim for a mix of lean breast meat and dark leg meat.*

BAKED PINTO BEANS

SERVES 8   Pintos are the bean of choice in the Lone Star State, and unlike baked beans in other parts of the country, they're generally not sweetened with any molasses or sugar. They're a delicious accompaniment to barbecue, along with sliced white bread and pickles.

2½ cups dried pinto beans

3 bacon slices

3½ cups low-sodium beef broth

¼ cup Texas Dry Rub (page 189)

⭐ *If you have some spare cooked brisket lying around, chop some up and drop it in for an extra layer of beefy flavor.*

1 Put the beans in a large bowl, cover with water, and set aside at room temperature to soak overnight.

2 Drain the beans and transfer them to a large ovenproof pot. Cover them with fresh water by 2 inches. Bring the water to a boil, reduce the heat to a simmer, and cook the beans for 30 to 35 minutes, or until tender. Drain and set aside.

3 Preheat the oven to 350°F.

4 Wipe out the pot and cook the bacon over high heat for 1½ to 2 minutes, or until crisp on one side. Reduce the heat to medium, turn the bacon, and cook the other side for 1 to 2 minutes more. Remove the bacon from the pot and set it aside. Do not drain the rendered fat from the pot.

5 Add the beans, beef broth, and Texas Dry Rub to the pot. Crumble in the bacon and stir everything to combine. Cover the pot and transfer it to the oven. Bake the beans for 70 to 80 minutes, or until the liquid has thickened.

MEAT MARKET PICKLES

★ PREP TIME: 10 MINUTES, PLUS 24 HOURS TO CHILL ★
COOK TIME: 5 MINUTES

Style: CENTRAL TEXAS

SERVES 6 Tangy pickles are the usual accompaniment to smoked sausage and brisket in Central Texas grocery stores and meat markets, such as Kreuz Market and Black's Barbecue, a tradition that dates back to the early twentieth century when German and Czech settlers arrived in the region.

1½ cups distilled white vinegar

½ cup water

2 tablespoons kosher salt

2 tablespoons sugar

2 cups sliced Kirby cucumbers

10 garlic cloves, smashed

2 tablespoons yellow mustard seeds

1 tablespoon black peppercorns

1 tablespoon coriander seeds

⭐ *If you plan on keeping the pickles longer than a few weeks, sterilize the jars and lids before using them by placing them in boiling water for 10 minutes. Then, after filling and sealing the jars, process them by placing them in boiling water for another 10 minutes, or until the lids pop down. Store them at room temperature in a cool, dark place and refrigerate only after opening.*

1 Thoroughly wash two wide-mouth pint jars and their lids in hot soapy water.

2 In a medium pot, combine the vinegar, water, salt, and sugar; bring it to a boil.

3 Divide the cucumbers, garlic, mustard seeds, peppercorns, and coriander seeds between the two jars and pour the hot brine into the jars. Leave a ½-inch space from the top of each jar (you may not need all the brine).

4 Cover the jars with their lids and tightly screw on the rings. Let the jars cool to room temperature and then refrigerate them for at least 24 hours.

PICKLED RED ONION

★ PREP TIME: 10 MINUTES, PLUS 1 HOUR TO CHILL ★
COOK TIME: 5 MINUTES

Style: TEXAS

SERVES 8 Pickled red onions are a wonderful addition to barbecue sandwiches. Their sweet-sour tang contrasts nicely with the fatty richness of the meat.

1½ cups distilled white vinegar

½ cup water

3 tablespoons sugar

2 tablespoons kosher salt

2 cups sliced red onion

2 tablespoons yellow mustard seeds

A mandoline makes quick work of slicing onions thinly and gives a nice, uniform cut; just make sure to use the hand guard.

1 Thoroughly wash two wide-mouth pint jars and their lids in hot soapy water.

2 In a medium pot, combine the vinegar, water, sugar, and salt; bring it to a boil.

3 Divide the onion and mustard seeds between the two jars and pour the hot brine into the jars. Leave a ½-inch space from the top of each container (you may not need all the brine).

4 Cover the jars with their lids and tightly screw on the rings. Let the jars cool to room temperature, then refrigerate them for at least 1 hour.

ESCABÈCHE

★ **PREP TIME: 10 MINUTES, PLUS 1 HOUR TO CHILL** ★
COOK TIME: 10 MINUTES

Style: SOUTH TEXAS

SERVES 8   Escabèche is a condiment that you're more likely to find at a taqueria than a barbecue joint, except when you're in South Texas, where the Mexican influence lends an interesting touch to the region's food.

1 cup distilled white vinegar

1 cup water

¼ cup kosher salt

3 tablespoons sugar

10 garlic cloves, crushed

1 cup sliced white onion

½ cup sliced jalapeño

½ cup sliced carrots

10 fresh cilantro sprigs

⭐ *Hot peppers contain a compound called capsaicin that can create a burning sensation on your skin. To protect yourself, consider wearing gloves when working with jalapeños and other chiles.*

1 Thoroughly wash two wide-mouth pint jars and their lids in hot soapy water.

2 In a medium pot, combine the vinegar, water, salt, and sugar; bring it to a boil.

3 Divide the garlic, onion, jalapeño, carrots, and cilantro between the two jars and pour the hot brine into the jars. Leave a ½-inch space from the top of each container (you may not need all the brine).

4 Cover the jars with the lids and tightly screw on the rings. Let the jars cool to room temperature and then refrigerate them for at least 1 hour.

JOHN TESAR

John Tesar is the owner of two highly acclaimed Dallas restaurants, Knife and Cut, and is an annual participant in Meatopia, a festival that brings together the world's best pitmasters in New York, Miami, and London. Learn more about John at www.chefjohntesar.com.

What aspects of barbecue appeal to you?

The ability to take something that's not considered expensive or elaborate and make it delicious, with or without smoke, appeals to me. I know a large part of barbecue is smoke, but I like to take some of those applications, remove the smoke, and do only the technique. For example, I'll sous-vide chuck short ribs at the same temperature you would barbecue them, slow and low, and then finish them over a red oak fire.

If you were to open a barbecue restaurant, what kind would it be?

I'd be like Aaron Franklin. I would serve brisket, sausage, and turkey, maybe a big rib. To me, brisket and sausage are the two most important components of barbecue.

Is buying USDA Prime beef overkill?

No, Prime is good. It's not just fat; it's texture. In a true Angus animal, the separation of the fat and protein creates texture, and they become one as they melt. When you render down Angus, the layers of fat and protein compress but stay stabilized.

Any advice on making sausage?

Before you put your meat into any kind of casing, continuously work on your mix of lean-to-fat and season it. I was taught in France that when you make pâté or forcemeat, you've got to cook a little of it, like a little hamburger disk, and taste it because after that, you're at the point of no return.

 In a true Angus animal, the separation of the fat and protein creates texture, and they become one as they melt.

JOHN TESAR'S SMOKED MERGUEZ SAUSAGE

PREP TIME: 3 HOURS ★ COOK TIME: 1½ HOURS

Style: **TEXAS**

SERVES 10 TO 12   For John Tesar, chef and partner at Dallas restaurants Knife and Oak, the art and craft of making sausage has always been a passion. When making sausage, he says it's important to have a style. "You're not reinventing sausage," he says. "It's been around for a thousand years."

2 teaspoons cumin seeds

2 teaspoons coriander seeds

2 teaspoons fennel seeds

2 tablespoons sweet paprika

2 tablespoons kosher salt

1 teaspoon cayenne pepper

3 pounds lamb shoulder, cut into ¾-inch cubes, gristle removed

1 pound lamb or pork fat, cut into ¾-inch cubes

2 tablespoons minced garlic

1 tablespoon red pepper flakes

⅓ cup ice water

Lamb casings, soaked in warm water for 30 minutes

★ *Before grinding the meat and fat, it's a good idea to chill the bowl of the stand mixer and the parts of the meat grinder in a big tub of ice or in the freezer.*

LEVEL OF DIFFICULTY
ADVANCED

RECOMMENDED WOOD
OAK OR PECAN

1 In a skillet, preferably cast iron, toast the cumin, coriander, and fennel seeds over medium heat until fragrant, about 2 minutes. Using a spice grinder, grind the toasted seeds into a fine powder, and transfer to a small bowl. Stir in the paprika, salt, and cayenne.

2 Combine the lamb and fat in a large bowl. Add the spice mixture, garlic, and red pepper flakes. Toss to thoroughly coat the meat and fat in the seasonings. Cover the bowl with plastic wrap and refrigerate until ready to grind the sausage.

3 Assemble your meat grinder according to the manufacturer's instructions, and fit it with the medium die. Grind the meat and fat mixture through the machine twice.

4 Transfer the grind to the bowl of a stand mixer fitted with the paddle attachment. Mix the sausage on low speed for 1 minute. Add the ice water and mix until the liquid is incorporated and the sausage is uniform and sticky, about 1 minute more.

➡➡

➔ JOHN TESAR'S SMOKED MERGUEZ SAUSAGE

5 Form a small sausage patty from the mixture and put the rest of the sausage mixture in the refrigerator. In a small frying pan over medium-high heat, cook the sausage patty until it is cooked through. Taste it and adjust the seasoning of the refrigerated sausage mixture if necessary.

6 Stuff the sausage into the lamb casings and twist them into 6-inch links. Refrigerate the links until chilled completely.

7 Preheat the smoker to the lowest temperature possible.

8 If using wood chips or chunks, soak them in water for at least 15 to 30 minutes. Add them to the smoker following the manufacturer's instructions.

9 Place a pan of ice in the smoker, and then place the sausages in the smoker over the ice and smoke them for 1 hour. Refrigerate the sausages until you're ready to finish cooking them.

10 To finish cooking the sausages, grill or sauté them until the internal temperature reaches 160°F.

CHIPOTLE SLAW

★ **PREP TIME: 15 MINUTES, PLUS 30 MINUTES TO CHILL** ★

Style: **CENTRAL TEXAS**

SERVES 4 Sometimes a departure from tradition is refreshing. Chipotles in adobo sauce give this slaw a savory, peppery kick—a nice change from traditional coleslaw.

2 teaspoons kosher salt

2 tablespoons distilled white vinegar

¼ cup canned chipotles in adobo, with liquid, finely chopped

¼ cup Homemade Mayonnaise (page 219) or store-bought

¼ head red cabbage, cored and thinly sliced

¼ head green cabbage, cored and thinly sliced

1 In a large bowl, whisk the salt into the vinegar until it dissolves. Add the chipotles in adobo and Homemade Mayonnaise and whisk until the ingredients are incorporated.

2 Add the red and green cabbage and toss until well coated. Refrigerate the slaw for at least 30 minutes before serving.

⭐ *Chipotles in adobo can be found in the international foods aisle of your supermarket.*

CENTRAL TEXAS COLESLAW

★ **PREP TIME: 15 MINUTES, PLUS 30 MINUTES TO CHILL** ★

Style: CENTRAL TEXAS

SERVES 4 Cool, crunchy slaw is a must-have accompaniment with Central Texas barbecue. The use of ground mustard is a hallmark of the German-Czech influence on the region's food.

2 teaspoons kosher salt

2 tablespoons apple cider vinegar

¼ cup Homemade Mayonnaise (page 219) or store-bought

2 teaspoons ground mustard

2 teaspoons freshly ground black pepper

¼ head red cabbage, cored and thinly sliced

¼ head green cabbage, cored and thinly sliced

1 In a large bowl, whisk the salt into the vinegar until it dissolves. Add the Homemade Mayonnaise, ground mustard, and pepper and whisk until the ingredients are incorporated.

2 Add the red and green cabbage and toss until well coated. Refrigerate the slaw for at least 30 minutes before serving.

⭐ *To cut down on prep work, look for bags of precut cabbage in the bagged salad section of your supermarket. Just be sure to wash it before using.*

GERMAN POTATO SALAD

PREP TIME: 5 MINUTES ★ COOK TIME: 20 MINUTES

Style: CENTRAL TEXAS

SERVES 4 Much of Central Texas barbecue traces its roots back to meat markets operated by German and Czech settlers to the region in the early twentieth century. Their limited offerings of smoked beef and sausage, pickles, plain bread, and sliced onion gradually expanded to incorporate items such as this potato salad, which is typical of the region's style. For a variation in flavor, try adding some sliced red onion or replace the Meat Market pickles with pickled jalapeño.

¼ cup Homemade Mayonnaise (page 219) or store-bought

2 tablespoons yellow mustard

1 tablespoon pickle juice

1 tablespoon sugar

1¼ pounds baby red and white potatoes, scrubbed

2 teaspoons kosher salt, plus more for the boiling water

½ cup chopped Meat Market Pickles (page 177) or store-bought dill pickles

⭐ *Leave the peels on the potatoes, but scrub them thoroughly before cooking to loosen any dirt.*

1 In a medium bowl, whisk together the Homemade Mayonnaise, mustard, pickle juice, sugar, and salt. Set aside.

2 Put the potatoes in a medium pot, cover with cold water by 1 inch, and salt the water until it tastes like the sea. Bring the water to a boil and cook the potatoes for 13 to 15 minutes, or until they are fork tender.

3 Drain the potatoes, let them cool to room temperature, and cut them into halves or quarters, depending on their size. Transfer them to the bowl with the dressing. Add the chopped Meat Market Pickles and toss everything to combine with the dressing. Serve immediately.

EASY MACARONI SALAD

PREP TIME: 10 MINUTES ★ **COOK TIME: 5 MINUTES**

Style: TEXAS

SERVES 4 Need a classic barbecue side dish that you can put together in just about no time? Who doesn't, especially after a 12-hour smoke job like a brisket. This classic macaroni salad is just the ticket.

Kosher salt

1½ cups dried macaroni

½ cup Homemade Mayonnaise (page 219) or store-bought

Juice of ¼ lemon

3 celery stalks with leaves, finely chopped

1 red bell pepper, seeded and finely chopped

Freshly ground black pepper

⭐ *If you're not going to use cooked pasta right away, toss it with a bit of olive oil to keep it from clumping up as it cools.*

1 Bring a medium pot of water to a boil and salt it until it tastes like the sea. Add the macaroni and cook it for 5 minutes, or until al dente. Drain and set aside.

2 In a medium bowl, whisk together the Homemade Mayonnaise and lemon juice. Add the macaroni, celery, and bell pepper and toss until the ingredients are well coated with the mayonnaise.

3 Season the salad with salt and pepper. Serve immediately.

TEXAS DRY RUB

PREP TIME: 10 MINUTES ★ COOK TIME: 2 MINUTES

Style: TEXAS

MAKES ABOUT ¾ CUP This rub is guaranteed to make your barbecue sing with flavor. In a nod to our neighbors south of the border, this dry rub makes generous use of various Mexican chiles in powdered form, which add a smoky complexity.

1 tablespoon cumin seeds

1 teaspoon black peppercorns

⅓ cup kosher salt

1 tablespoon smoked Spanish paprika

1 tablespoon sweet Spanish paprika

4 teaspoons ground ancho chile

2 teaspoons ground chipotle chile

1 teaspoon ground guajillo chile

1 teaspoon dried oregano, preferably Mexican

1 teaspoon turbinado sugar

1 In a small sauté pan, toast the cumin seeds and black peppercorns over medium heat for 1 to 2 minutes, or until fragrant. Let them cool and then blend them thoroughly in a spice grinder. Transfer the grind to a small bowl.

2 Add the salt, smoked paprika, sweet paprika, ground ancho chile, ground chipotle chile, ground guajillo chile, oregano, and sugar. Mix thoroughly to combine. Store the rub in an airtight container.

⭐ *Letting toasted spices cool to room temperature before grinding them prevents them from steaming inside the grinder and sticking to the sides.*

COFFEE-CHILI DRY RUB

★ **PREP TIME: 1 MINUTE** ★

Style: **TEXAS**

MAKES ABOUT ¼ CUP   The complex, deep flavors of this dry rub stand up well to rich cuts of beef like brisket. If you happen to have some espresso powder lying around, feel free to use it, but instant coffee does a fantastic job at a fraction of the cost. The important thing is to make sure that whatever coffee you use is fresh.

1 tablespoon instant coffee
1 tablespoon turbinado sugar
1 tablespoon ground ancho chile
1 teaspoon ground chipotle chile
1 teaspoon ground guajillo chile
2 teaspoons kosher salt

In a small bowl, stir together all the ingredients, and transfer to an airtight container for storage.

⭐ *Dry rubs will keep in a cool, dark place for up to 6 months.*

EAST TEXAS BARBECUE SAUCE

★ PREP TIME: 5 MINUTES ★
COOK TIME: 5 MINUTES, PLUS OVERNIGHT TO CHILL

Style: EAST TEXAS

MAKES ABOUT 1 CUP Toasted cumin and smoked paprika are what give this barbecue sauce its smokiness, while the ground chiles add notes of coffee, fruitiness, and tang.

1 tablespoon cumin seeds

7 teaspoons smoked Spanish paprika

1 tablespoon sweet Spanish paprika

1 tablespoon ground ancho chile

1 teaspoon ground chipotle chile

1 teaspoon ground guajillo chile

1 teaspoon cayenne pepper

1 teaspoon dried oregano, preferably Mexican

1 teaspoon kosher salt

1 cup ketchup

½ cup distilled white vinegar

6 tablespoons brown sugar

2 tablespoons vegetable oil

⭐ *Cumin seeds will start to pop when they're toasted through.*

1 In a small sauté pan, toast the cumin seeds over medium heat for 1 to 2 minutes, or until fragrant. Let them cool and then blend them thoroughly in a spice grinder. Transfer the grind to a small bowl.

2 Add the smoked paprika, sweet paprika, ground ancho chile, ground chipotle chile, ground guajillo chile, cayenne, oregano, and salt. Mix thoroughly to combine and set aside.

3 In a medium bowl, whisk together the ketchup, vinegar, and brown sugar to create the wet mixture. Set aside.

4 In a medium saucepan, heat the oil over medium heat.

5 Add the spice mixture and cook it for 10 seconds, or until fragrant.

6 Stir in the wet mixture and simmer everything for about 1 minute, or until the flavors meld.

7 Let the sauce cool and then refrigerate it overnight before using.

WILLIAM WEISIGER

William Weisiger is the head pitmaster at Ten 50 BBQ in Dallas. Learn more about their barbecue at www.ten50bbq.com.

Tell us a little bit about your history as a professional pitmaster.

I learned to smoke from my grandfather and great uncle. That grew into a passion for smoking meat. Although earlier on I took a different career path, I've always had barbecue on my mind. So a few years back, I started smoking for friends and family, which led to more "friends" who wanted to eat barbecue. Eventually, this path led me to Ten 50 BBQ.

Describe the setup you have at the restaurant.

We use Oyler pits built by J&R Manufacturing in Mesquite, Texas. We burn post oak and hickory using indirect heat.

What are your thoughts on wrapping? Is it a useful technique?

I think wrapping is a great technique. It aids in the cooking process, retaining moisture and protecting the bark.

When purchasing brisket, how important is marbling?

Marbling is very important in any cut of beef, especially a brisket. I personally prefer Upper Choice or Prime to produce a succulent piece of beef.

What are your thoughts on the future of barbecue in America?

As barbecue's popularity rises, I think there will continue to be a blending of regional styles, focusing on higher grades of meat. Also, there will be more cross-over into fine dining.

 A few years back, I started smoking for friends and family, which led to more "friends" who wanted to eat barbecue.

WILLIAM WEISIGER'S TEXAS-STYLE BRISKET

★ **PREP TIME: 1 HOUR** ★

COOK TIME: 10 TO 12 HOURS, PLUS 1 HOUR TO REST

Style: TEXAS

SERVES: 10 TO 14 William Weisiger, head pitmaster of Ten 50 BBQ in Dallas, shares his recipe for Texas-style brisket. He recommends using an offset barrel smoker and post oak wood for the most authentic experience.

FOR THE ROASTED GARLIC

2 cups peeled garlic cloves

4 cups vegetable oil

FOR THE BRISKET

½ cup kosher salt

½ cup coarsely ground black pepper

1 (10- to 14-pound) whole packer brisket, USDA Choice or better

Vegetable oil, for brushing the grates

⭐ *The smoke ring is the benchmark by which brisket is judged. To get a good smoke ring, start with a brisket that is cooler than room temperature (this gives more time for the ring to develop) and use wood that is not overly seasoned.*

LEVEL OF DIFFICULTY

ADVANCED

RECOMMENDED WOOD

POST OAK

TO MAKE THE ROASTED GARLIC

1 In a medium saucepan, combine the garlic cloves and vegetable oil.

2 Bring to a simmer over low heat and cook for 20 to 30 minutes, or until golden brown and fragrant.

3 Remove from the heat and let cool to room temperature. Refrigerate any unused garlic cloves in the oil in an airtight container for up to 1 month.

TO MAKE THE BRISKET

1 In a small bowl, mix together the salt, pepper, and 3 tablespoons of minced roasted garlic.

2 Trim the brisket fat cap to ¼-inch thickness. Season the brisket with the rub. Let the meat stand at room temperature for 1 hour before smoking.

3 Preheat the smoker to 225°F.

4 If using wood chips or chunks, soak them in water for at least 15 to 30 minutes. Add them to the smoker following the manufacturer's instructions.

➤➤ WILLIAM WEISIGER'S TEXAS-STYLE BRISKET

5 Oil the smoker grates and place the brisket on them, fat-side up. Close the cooking compartment and cook the meat for 10 to 12 hours, or until the internal temperature reaches 190°F to 195°F. Rotate the brisket every 2 to 3 hours while it cooks. Add wood and fuel as necessary to maintain the smoke and temperature in the smoker.

6 Remove the brisket from the smoker and let it rest for 1 hour. To serve, slice the brisket against the grain into ¼-inch-thick slices.

TEXAS TOAST

Style: TEXAS

SERVES 4 Texas toast is a type of packaged bread that's sold throughout the state (and in the frozen food section of most supermarkets country-wide). When served as an accompaniment to barbecue, it's sliced very thick and is usually buttered and toasted with a hint of garlic.

6 garlic cloves, minced

6 tablespoons unsalted butter, at room temperature

4 (1-inch-thick) slices white bread

⭐ *To soften butter quickly, cut it into small chunks and place it in a microwave-safe dish. Microwave on the defrost setting for 10 to 15 seconds at a time until softened but not melted.*

1 Preheat the broiler.

2 In a small bowl, fold the garlic into the butter.

3 Spread the mixture on both sides of each slice of bread.

4 Place the bread under the broiler for 2 to 3 minutes on each side, or until it is light golden brown on both sides.

THE REST
OF THE U.S.

After a trip through the four major barbecue regions—the Carolinas, Memphis, Kansas City, and Texas—it may seem like the journey is over. But, actually, it's really just beginning. There are plenty of other places with their own barbecue traditions that are definitely worth exploring. Here's a brief look at some of the most interesting ones.

PROTEINS

Alabama. Pork ribs and chopped or sliced pork shoulder, smoked with hickory or pecan, are the staples. Some places do brisket, too, but the most interesting tradition comes from the northern part of the state, where smoked chicken is served with a white barbecue sauce.

California. California is famous for the Santa Maria tri-tip, a pyramid-shape cut of beef taken from the top of the sirloin, created by a butcher named Bob Schutz in the 1950s. Although the modern-day barbecue version of the Santa Maria style is closer to grilling, the original concept involved placing cuts of beef on a spit over red oak. Michael Ollier, corporate chef for Certified Angus Beef, shares a recipe for Santa Maria tri-tip that harks back to the original method.

Georgia. In Georgia, most places echo the traditions of the Carolinas, with whole hogs or pork butts cooked in a pit using oak or hickory.

Kentucky. Kentucky's claim to fame lies in the western part of the state, where they serve barbecued mutton. The tradition is especially strong in Owensboro, where four restaurants serve it.

Mississippi. In Mississippi, pork shoulder is sliced cold, heated up on a flat top, and chopped up before being tossed in barbecue sauce and piled on a bun.

FLAVORS, RUBS, AND SAUCES

Alabama. Alabama is known for its white barbecue sauce, invented by Bob Gibson, who began barbecuing on the weekends as a hobby in the 1920s. His business has since grown and expanded into a thriving restaurant, and this mayonnaise-based sauce has traveled far beyond its northern Alabama roots.

California. The Santa Maria rub highlights the flavor of beef. Ollier's version is a simple mixture of salt, pepper, honey, garlic powder, and onion powder.

Georgia. Seasoning tends to be just salt and pepper, if that, and sauces are based on ketchup and molasses.

Kentucky. In Western Kentucky, a black barbecue sauce made with Worcestershire, vinegar, lemon juice, and allspice is the traditional accompaniment to barbecued mutton. The allspice is an important ingredient because it helps cut through the gaminess of the meat.

Mississippi. In Mississippi, sauces are rich, thick, and dark red, made from a ketchup base and sweetened with plenty of brown sugar.

FILL THE PLATE

Alabama. Most places just stick to slaw and beans, but if you're lucky enough to find a place that goes the extra mile, expect a nice Southern spread with everything from pimiento cheese to collard greens.

California. The traditional accompaniments to Santa Maria barbecue include pinquito beans, grilled buttered bread, a green salad, and salsa.

Georgia. Georgia's best-known side dish is Brunswick stew, versions of which also exist in Virginia and North Carolina. The Georgia version has a variety of meats, including pork, beef, or chicken, plus corn, potatoes, lima beans, and tomatoes. It is simmered until thick and the meats are fork tender.

Kentucky. Kentucky also has its own stew, called burgoo. There are many different versions, but the most interesting one is by James T. Looney, one of the so-called "Burgoo Kings." His version is seasoned with curry powder, Angostura bitters, and Worcestershire sauce, an unlikely combination that works surprisingly well.

Mississippi. Slaw and baked beans are must-haves, but interestingly, a few places serve boiled hot tamales.

POPULAR PAIRINGS

Throughout the South, you really can't go wrong with sweet tea, and if you're feeling something a bit boozier, an easygoing pilsner, lager, or even hefeweizen are good choices. In California, it's not unusual to serve a big, bold red wine that can stand up to beef.

POINTS TO REMEMBER

★ **Stir that stew.** Many of the stew and gravy-like dishes are pretty low maintenance for the most part, but it's important to stir them more often as you approach the end of cooking and as they start to really thicken. You definitely don't want to scorch the bottom of the pan.

★ **Egg safety.** Whenever you use raw eggs to make dressings or condiments, there is always a slight risk of foodborne illness. To minimize the risk, use the freshest eggs possible or buy pasteurized eggs.

★ **Lamb or mutton?** Mutton can be difficult to find, even if you have access to a good butcher. Lamb can be smoked, too, with delicious results. Opt for bone-in legs or shoulders and aim for an internal temperature of 190°F for tender meat. Consider wrapping the meat once it gets enough color and smoke to keep it moist while it finishes cooking.

★ **Chopping or slicing?** Shoulders (including the butt and picnic) should be cooked to 185°F if slicing or chopping or 190°F if pulling.

★ **Let it cool.** Allowing meat to rest for at least 1 hour before slicing allows the juices to redistribute back into the meat and prevents them from leaking out when you carve the meat.

BEER CAN CHICKEN

★ PREP TIME: 1 HOUR ★

COOK TIME: 3 TO 4 HOURS, PLUS 1 HOUR TO REST

Style: NORTHERN ALABAMA

SERVES 4   Beer can chicken is sheer genius, and a classic. The beer evaporates and moistens the interior as the chicken cooks, making the meat juicy.

1 (4- to 5-pound) whole chicken

⅓ cup Poultry Dry Rub (page 220)

1 can American lager, such as Budweiser, half empty

2 tablespoons vegetable oil, for brushing the grates

⭐ *If the chicken refuses to stand, open up a couple more cans, drink some of the beer, and use them to prop it up.*

LEVEL OF DIFFICULTY
BEGINNER

RECOMMENDED WOOD
APPLE

1 Season the chicken with the Poultry Dry Rub and let stand at room temperature for 1 hour.

2 Preheat the smoker to 225°F to 250°F.

3 If using wood chips or chunks, soak them in water for at least 15 to 30 minutes. Add them to the smoker following the manufacturer's instructions.

4 Oil the smoker grates. Insert the half-full beer can into the cavity of the chicken and place it upright inside the smoker, using the beer can as a stand. Close the cooking compartment and smoke the chicken for 3 to 4 hours, or until an instant-read thermometer inserted without touching the bone reads 160°F. Add wood and fuel as necessary to maintain the smoke and temperature in the smoker.

5 Remove the chicken from the smoker and let it rest for 1 hour. Carve off the breasts, thighs, and legs and serve.

MICHAEL OLLIER

Michael Ollier is the corporate executive chef for the Certified Angus Beef brand. Learn more about him and the Certified Angus Beef brand at www.gorare.com.

How did you first become interested in barbecue?

While I've long had an appreciation for really good 'cue, I became totally enamored of smoking and barbecue during a visit to Austin in 2012. As part of an IACP [International Association of Culinary Professionals] conference, I participated in a Central Texas barbecue tour. It has been a smoking love affair ever since.

Please describe your signature barbecue style.

I'm a staunch believer that food doesn't have to be complex or pretentious to be delicious. My philosophy is: If you start with the best ingredients you can afford, and prepare them with care, you will have success.

What's the most interesting project you've worked on lately?

Sometimes a challenge, but always an intriguing one in my line of work, is the regionality of beef cuts' names, uses, and flavors. One notable example: Tri-tip is a cut from the bottom sirloin that Californians have long adored. Once new to Midwesterners like myself, I have since fallen under its spell as well. While staying true to the traditional grilling technique of Santa Maria tri-tip (think serious char on a 3-pound hunk of juicy beef), I have added smoke to the equation, combining my two favorite techniques: true low-and-slow wood-smoked barbecue, and direct heat grilling.

 My philosophy is: If you start with the best ingredients you can afford, and prepare them with care, you will have success.

SMOKED AND GRILLED SANTA MARIA TRI-TIP

★ PREP TIME: 20 TO 30 MINUTES, PLUS 2 HOURS TO MARINATE ★
COOK TIME: 1½ HOURS

Style: CALIFORNIA

SERVES 8 TO 10 Although smoking and grilling lie at opposite ends of the spectrum of outdoor cooking, when you're working with the right cut of meat, the two techniques can be combined with spectacular results. This tri-tip is a great example of that.

1 (3-pound) tri-tip roast
3 to 4 tablespoons Santa Maria Rub
  (page 221)
Vegetable oil, for brushing the grates

⭐ *It's a good idea to replace your grill brush regularly. Over time, the metal bristles can fall out—definitely something you don't want to end up in your food.*

LEVEL OF DIFFICULTY
INTERMEDIATE

RECOMMENDED WOOD
RED OAK

1 Evenly rub the tri-tip with the Santa Maria Rub. Wrap it tightly in plastic or a resealable bag. Refrigerate it for at least 2 hours, or overnight for a more intense flavor.

2 Preheat the smoker to 215°F.

3 If using wood chips or chunks, soak them in water for at least 15 to 30 minutes. Add them to the smoker following the manufacturer's instructions.

4 Oil the smoker grates and place the tri-tip on them. Close the cooking compartment and smoke the meat for 1 hour, or until an instant-read thermometer reads 120°F. Add wood and fuel as necessary to maintain the smoke and temperature in the smoker.

➤ SMOKED AND GRILLED SANTA MARIA TRI-TIP

5 After 1 hour in the smoker, move the tri-tip to either a grill or a stove-top grill pan. If using a grill, give yourself enough time to preheat the grill to achieve medium-high heat. If using a grill pan on the stove top, heat it to medium-high heat. Transfer the tri-tip to the grill or grill pan and grill it on each side to develop a dark crust, reaching an internal temperature of 130°F to 135°F, about 10 minutes per side.

6 Move the meat to a cutting board, tent aluminum foil over it, and let the meat rest for 10 minutes. Slice the meat thinly against the grain and serve.

WESTERN KENTUCKY BARBECUED LAMB

★ PREP TIME: 1 HOUR ★
COOK TIME: 7½ TO 9 HOURS, PLUS 1 HOUR TO REST

Style: KENTUCKY

SERVES 8 Barbecuing lamb is an underappreciated method for its preparation. The gaminess of the meat mellows out through the low and slow smoking process. In Western Kentucky, barbecue restaurants specialize in smoked mutton served with Black Barbecue Sauce (page 224). Mutton can be hard to find, but lamb works just as well.

1 (5- to 6-pound) bone-in leg of lamb
2 tablespoons kosher salt
2 tablespoons freshly ground black pepper
Vegetable oil, for brushing the grates

⭐ *Open the smoker only when absolutely necessary. Each time you lift the lid, it adds about 15 minutes to the cooking time.*

LEVEL OF DIFFICULTY
BEGINNER

RECOMMENDED WOOD
HICKORY

1 Trim the fat from the lamb and season it with the salt and pepper (see page 44). Let it stand at room temperature for 1 hour.

2 Preheat the smoker to 225°F to 275°F.

3 If using wood chips or chunks, soak them in water for at least 15 to 30 minutes. Add them to the smoker following the manufacturer's instructions.

4 Oil the smoker grates and place the lamb on them, fat-side up. Close the cooking compartment and smoke the meat for 7½ to 9 hours, or until an instant-read thermometer inserted without touching the bone reads 190°F. Add wood and fuel as necessary to maintain the smoke and temperature in the smoker.

5 Remove the lamb from the smoker and let it rest for 1 hour. Discard the bones and slice or chop the meat to serve.

MISSISSIPPI-STYLE SMOKED BOSTON BUTT

★ **PREP TIME: 1 HOUR** ★
COOK TIME: 9 TO 10 HOURS, PLUS OVERNIGHT TO CHILL

Style: **MISSISSIPPI**

SERVES 12　In Mississippi, pork shoulder is served very differently than in other parts of the country. It's chilled overnight after cooking, sliced very thinly the next day, and heated up on a grill or griddle.

1 (7- to 8-pound) bone-in Boston butt
3 tablespoons kosher salt
3 tablespoons freshly ground black pepper
Vegetable oil, for brushing the grates
Mississippi-Style Barbecue Sauce (page 225), for serving

⭐ *Whenever you plan on slicing your pork shoulder instead of chopping or pulling it, cook it to a slightly lower internal temperature than usual—185°F instead of 190°F—which will keep the meat a bit firmer once it's done cooking.*

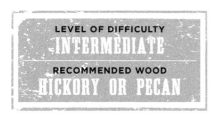

LEVEL OF DIFFICULTY
INTERMEDIATE
RECOMMENDED WOOD
HICKORY OR PECAN

1 Trim the fat from the butt and season it with the salt and pepper (see page 39). Let it stand at room temperature for 1 hour.

2 Preheat the smoker to 225°F to 275°F. If using wood chips, soak them in water for 15 to 30 minutes. Add them to the smoker following the manufacturer's instructions.

3 Oil the smoker grates and place the butt on them. Close the cooking compartment and cook the meat for 7 to 7½ hours, or until an instant-read thermometer inserted without touching the bone reads 165°F. At this point you can wrap the meat in aluminum foil if you think it will lose too much moisture as it cooks. Add wood and fuel as necessary to maintain the smoke and temperature.

4 Turn over the butt and continue cooking it for 2 to 2¼ hours, or until the internal temperature reaches 185°F.

5 Remove the butt from the smoker, remove the foil (if used), and let it cool to room temperature. Wrap it tightly in plastic to keep the meat moist and refrigerate it overnight.

6 Thinly slice the meat and place the slices on a hot grill or griddle until they are heated through and charred in spots. Serve with the Mississippi-Style Barbecue Sauce.

MISSISSIPPI-STYLE SLICED PORK SANDWICH

★ **PREP TIME: 5 MINUTES** ★

Style: **MISSISSIPPI**

SERVES 4 Order a pork sandwich at a typical joint in Mississippi, and you'll get something that's a little bit different than what you would find elsewhere in the South. There, chilled pork shoulder is sliced thinly and placed on a grill to give each slice a nice char, then tossed in a thick, red sauce.

1 pound thinly sliced pork from Mississippi-Style Smoked Boston Butt (page 206)

4 white hamburger buns

¼ cup unsalted butter, at room temperature

1 cup Mississippi-Style Barbecue Sauce (page 225)

2 cups favorite coleslaw

⭐ *Avoid coating the pork slices with the sauce before putting them on the grill because the sauce contains a lot of sugar, which can burn and leave a bitter aftertaste.*

1 Prepare a grill for medium-high heat cooking, about 400°F.

2 Place the pork slices on the hot grill until they are heated through.

3 Meanwhile, slather the inside of the buns with the butter and place them butter-side down on the cool section of the grill to toast.

4 In a medium bowl, toss the charred pork slices with the Mississippi-Style Barbecue Sauce until it is thoroughly coated.

5 Place some pork on the toasted side heel of each bun. Mound some coleslaw on top of the pork and then crown the sandwich with the top of the bun.

DAVID AND JOE MALUFF

David and Joe Maluff are the owners of Full Moon Bar-B-Que, which has been dedicated to making Alabama barbecue using hickory wood over an open flame pit since 1986. Learn more at www.fullmoonbbq.com.

How would you say barbecue in Alabama has changed over the past 10 years?

The way customers prefer their 'cue served has changed. Nowadays, almost everyone orders their meat either chopped or pulled, but now and then there will be an old-school barbecue lover that likes their pork or brisket sliced. Barbecue connoisseurs want the "bark," the burnt part on the outside of the pork butt. You only get the bark when using hickory wood and an open flame pit.

What is your most popular item?

Our most popular item is our famous chow-chow. Chow-chow is a spicy, sweet organic relish that is a staple in Southern kitchens and a source of fierce (and usually friendly) competition at county fairs. It has become a Full Moon Bar-B-Que staple and offers barbecue lovers a crunchy, zingy alternative to the traditional topping or side. We are the only barbecue restaurant in the southern region that serves it.

Tell us about your pit setup.

Each of our Full Moon locations is built with a brick 30-by-15-foot wood-fired pit. Our pitmasters know exactly what temperature the pit needs to be to cook meats low and slow over the direct flame.

 Barbecue connoisseurs want the "bark," the burnt part on the outside of the pork butt. You only get the bark when using hickory wood and an open flame pit.

FULL MOON BAR-B-QUE'S MACARONI AND CHEESE

PREP TIME: 5 MINUTES ★ **COOK TIME: 30 MINUTES**

Style: ALABAMA

SERVES 8 TO 10   In the mood for some classic macaroni and cheese? This easy, simple version from Full Moon Bar-B-Que is always a customer favorite.

1 cup whole milk
½ cup (1 stick) solid margarine
Pinch kosher salt
Pinch freshly ground white pepper
1 cup shredded American cheese
3 cups cooked elbow macaroni

⭐ *To keep the pasta from sticking, boil it in plenty of salted water and stir it right after adding the noodles to the boiling water.*

1 Preheat the oven to 350°F.

2 In a medium pot, bring the milk to a boil. Add the margarine, salt, and white pepper. Reduce the heat to medium and, once the margarine has melted, slowly add the cheese while stirring constantly. Add the macaroni, stirring until it is fully coated in the cheese.

3 Transfer the macaroni and cheese to a 2-quart baking dish. Cover the dish and bake the macaroni and cheese for 25 minutes, or until the top is golden brown.

FULL MOON BAR-B-QUE'S COLLARD GREENS

PREP TIME: 5 MINUTES ★ COOK TIME: 3 HOURS

Style: ALABAMA

SERVES 4 The next time you smoke a whole turkey, save the wings for this delicious take on collard greens.

3 cups low-sodium chicken broth
1 large white onion, diced
8 ounces smoked turkey wings
1 bunch collard greens

⭐ *Wash collard greens thoroughly in a bowl under cool, running water. Agitate the greens to loosen any dirt, then let them sit undisturbed for about 10 minutes to allow the dirt to settle to the bottom.*

1 In a large pot, combine the chicken broth, onion, and turkey wings. Bring the liquid to a boil and then add the collards.

2 Reduce the heat to a simmer and cook the greens for 3 hours. Discard the turkey wings.

3 Transfer the greens to an appropriate container and let them cool for a couple of minutes before serving.

FULL MOON BAR-B-QUE'S MARINATED SLAW

Style: **ALABAMA**

SERVES 12   Here's a slaw recipe that will feed a hungry crowd. Pimiento peppers give this slaw its beautiful color and lend it a unique Southern touch.

1 head cabbage, cored and shredded

1 large green bell pepper, seeded and chopped

1 medium onion, finely chopped

1 celery stalk, chopped

1½ cups plus 1 tablespoon sugar, divided

1 cup vegetable oil

1 cup apple cider vinegar

1 tablespoon kosher salt

1 tablespoon chopped pimiento peppers

1 In a very large bowl, combine the cabbage, bell pepper, onion, and celery. Coat the vegetables with 1½ cups of sugar. Mix well.

2 In a saucepan, combine the oil, vinegar, salt, and remaining 1 tablespoon of sugar. Bring it to a boil, stirring constantly.

3 Pour the hot liquid over the shredded cabbage. Add the pimientos to the bowl and mix until everything is well combined.

4 Let the slaw cool, cover, and refrigerate until well chilled.

⭐ *The longer you allow slaw to marinate in the refrigerator, the more its flavor will improve.*

MUSTARD SLAW

Style: **ALABAMA**

SERVES 4 The mustard-and-vinegar dressing in this slaw packs plenty of punch to cut through the richness of pork ribs and shoulder, just what you need between bites of perfectly smoked barbecue.

2 teaspoons kosher salt

1 teaspoon sugar

1 teaspoon ground mustard

¼ cup apple cider vinegar

3 tablespoons yellow mustard

¼ head red cabbage, cored and thinly sliced

¼ head green cabbage, cored and thinly sliced

1 In a large bowl, whisk the salt, sugar, and ground mustard into the vinegar until they dissolve. Add the yellow mustard and whisk until it is well incorporated.

2 Add the red and green cabbage and toss until well coated by the dressing.

3 Refrigerate the slaw for at least 30 minutes before serving.

⭐ *Ground mustard packs a bit of heat along with its tanginess. Colman's is a popular brand.*

FULL MOON BAR-B-QUE'S PIMIENTO CHEESE

★ **PREP TIME: 10 MINUTES** ★

Style: **ALABAMA**

SERVES 4   This iconic dip is a staple in the South and a fantastic accompaniment to barbecue. You know you're in the South if you see a pimiento cheese sandwich on the menu.

1 cup shredded sharp Cheddar cheese

1 cup shredded extra-sharp Cheddar cheese

½ cup Homemade Mayonnaise (page 219) or store-bought

1 (8-ounce) jar chopped pimiento peppers, drained

½ cup diced jalapeños

In a medium bowl, combine the cheeses, Homemade Mayonnaise, pimiento peppers, and jalapeños. Mash everything with a fork and then stir the mixture with a rubber spatula until thoroughly mixed.

⭐ *A food processor fitted with the grater attachment can make quick work of shredding cheese. Cut the cheese into pieces small enough to insert into the feeder.*

GEORGIA-STYLE BRUNSWICK STEW

PREP TIME: 15 MINUTES ★ **COOK TIME: 4½ HOURS**

Style: GEORGIA

SERVES 8 Georgia-style Brunswick stew has three types of meat—chicken, pork, and beef—each cooked separately and then stewed. Talk about a meat-lover's delight.

3 bacon slices

8 ounces boneless, skinless chicken thighs, diced

8 ounces beef stew meat from the chuck

8 ounces pork stew meat

2 large yellow or white onions, diced

½ cup (1 stick) unsalted butter

½ cup all-purpose flour

1 (28-ounce) can crushed tomatoes

1 pound Yukon Gold potatoes, scrubbed and diced

2 cups fresh or frozen corn kernels, thawed if frozen

2 cups frozen lima beans, thawed

8 cups water

Kosher salt

Freshly ground black pepper

1 teaspoon cayenne pepper

⭐ *When browning meat, avoid crowding the pan, which will cause the meat to steam instead of sear.*

1 In a large pot, cook the bacon over high heat for 1½ to 2 minutes, or until crisp on one side. Reduce the heat to medium, turn the bacon, and cook the other side for 1 to 2 minutes more. Remove the bacon from the pot and set it aside. Do not drain the rendered fat from the pot.

2 Increase the heat to high and brown each of the meats separately, in batches if necessary, until a nice crust forms on each piece. Remove the meat from the pot and set it aside.

3 Reduce the heat to medium-high and add the onions to the pot. Sauté them for 5 to 7 minutes, or until softened.

4 Melt the butter in the pot. Add the flour, reduce the heat to low, and whisk it continuously for 3 to 5 minutes, or until smooth and light brown.

5 Return the meat to the pot along with the tomatoes, potatoes, corn, lima beans, and water; bring the liquid to a simmer. Crumble the bacon into the pot.

6 Season the stew with salt, black pepper, and the cayenne and bring the liquid to a boil. Then reduce the heat to a simmer and cook the stew for 4 hours, stirring occasionally, or until it has thickened. Serve immediately.

JAUBERT'S KENTUCKY BURGOO

PREP TIME: 15 MINUTES ★ COOK TIME: 4 HOURS

Style: KENTUCKY

SERVES 8 Gus Jaubert was the original "Burgoo King," and the invention of the dish is widely credited to him. He was also a very talented pitmaster. This burgoo recipe is inspired by his version of the dish.

3 bacon slices

2 large yellow or white onions, diced

½ cup (1 stick) unsalted butter

1 (1-pound) bone-in beef shank

1 pound boneless, skinless chicken thighs, diced

1 (28-ounce) can crushed tomatoes

1 pound Yukon Gold potatoes, scrubbed and diced

1 cup fresh or frozen corn kernels, thawed if frozen

4 quarts water

1 tablespoon kosher salt

1 tablespoon freshly ground black pepper

⭐ *Chuck is also a great choice for making this stew.*

1 In a large pot, cook the bacon over high heat for 1½ to 2 minutes, or until crisp on one side. Reduce the heat to medium, turn the bacon, and cook the other side for 1 to 2 minutes. Remove the bacon from the pot and set it aside. Do not drain the rendered fat from the pot.

2 Increase the heat to medium-high, add the onions to the pot, and sauté them for 6 to 7 minutes, or until slightly softened.

3 Add the butter, beef, chicken, tomatoes, potatoes, corn, and water to the pot and bring the liquid to a simmer. Crumble the bacon into the pot.

4 Season the burgoo with the salt and pepper and bring everything to a boil. Reduce the heat to a simmer and cook the burgoo, stirring more frequently toward the end of the cooking time, for 3½ hours, or until the beef separates easily from the bone and is tender. Serve immediately.

LOONEY'S KENTUCKY BURGOO

PREP TIME: 15 MINUTES ★ **COOK TIME: 4 HOURS**

Style: KENTUCKY

SERVES 8   Before his death in the 1920s, Gus Jaubert passed on his knowledge about burgoo to James T. Looney, who gladly took over the "Burgoo King" title and was a fixture of the Lexington barbecue scene, cooking at many horse races and political events. This recipe is inspired by his version of the dish.

2 tablespoons vegetable oil

1 (1½-pound) bone-in beef shank

8 ounces boneless, skinless chicken
  thighs, diced

1 cup dry sherry

8 ounces carrots, chopped

2 (15-ounce) cans diced tomatoes, undrained

8 ounces fresh or frozen corn, thawed
  if frozen

8 ounces shredded cabbage

8 cups water

¼ cup Worcestershire sauce

¼ cup ketchup

1 teaspoon Angostura bitters

1 tablespoon red pepper flakes

1 tablespoon curry powder

1 tablespoon kosher salt

2 teaspoons freshly ground black pepper

⭐ *Angostura bitters is a type of alcohol-based seasoning flavored with botanicals. You can find it in the condiments or mixers aisle of your supermarket.*

1 In a large pot, heat the oil over high heat. When it is hot, add the beef and chicken in a single layer, working in batches if necessary, and sear each piece on all sides, 8 to 10 minutes, or until browned. Remove the meat and set it aside.

2 Take the pot off the heat and deglaze the bottom by adding the sherry and gently scraping the bottom of the pan to loosen any meat and juices left behind. Place the pot back over high heat and bring the liquid to a boil.

3 When the sherry has reduced by half, about 3 to 4 minutes, return the meat to the pot, along with the carrots, tomatoes with their juices, corn, cabbage, and water. Season everything with the Worcestershire sauce, ketchup, bitters, red pepper flakes, curry powder, salt, and black pepper.

4 Reduce the heat to a simmer and cook the burgoo, stirring more frequently toward the end of the cooking time, for 3½ hours, or until the beef separates easily from the bone and is tender. Serve immediately.

"SWEET HOME ALABAMA" BARBECUE SAUCE

★ PREP TIME: 5 MINUTES ★

Style: NORTHERN ALABAMA

MAKES ABOUT 1½ CUPS If you've never had Alabama white sauce before, the use of mayonnaise as a base may seem a bit unusual. However, this classic sauce is a must-have with any barbecued chicken dish, and one bite will make you a true believer. Just try to save some for everyone else at the table.

1 cup Homemade Mayonnaise (page 219) or store-bought
¼ cup apple cider vinegar
1 jalapeño, seeded and finely diced
1 teaspoon kosher salt
1 teaspoon cayenne pepper

1 In a small bowl, whisk together the Homemade Mayonnaise, vinegar, jalapeño, salt, and cayenne.

2 Use the sauce immediately or transfer it to an airtight container and refrigerate for up to 1 week.

⭐ *To remove the seeds from a jalapeño, slice off the stem and cut the pepper in half lengthwise. Use the tip of the knife to scrape out the seeds.*

HOMEMADE MAYONNAISE

★ **PREP TIME: 10 MINUTES** ★

Style: AMERICAN

MAKES ABOUT 2 CUPS Store-bought mayonnaise is all well and good, but if you're looking to go the extra mile, homemade mayonnaise is worth the effort. If you've never made it before, you'll be surprised at just how simple it is to make. Once you master the technique, you can get creative and flavor it with just about any fresh herb or spice.

2 large eggs
2 cups vegetable oil
Pinch kosher salt

⭐ *Homemade mayonnaise will keep in the refrigerator for up to 5 days.*

1 In the bowl of a small food processor, process the eggs just until the yolks dissolve.

2 With the machine running, slowly drizzle in the oil until the mixture is thickened and resembles mayonnaise. Season with the salt.

3 Use the mayonnaise immediately or store it in an airtight container in the refrigerator.

POULTRY DRY RUB

PREP TIME: 2 MINUTES ★ **COOK TIME: 3 MINUTES**

Style: AMERICAN

MAKES ABOUT ⅓ CUP   Here's an all-purpose poultry rub that's equally at home on chicken, Cornish hens, and turkey.

1 tablespoon cumin seeds

1 teaspoon coriander seeds

1 teaspoon yellow mustard seeds

1 teaspoon black peppercorns

¼ cup kosher salt

1 tablespoon sweet paprika

1 tablespoon turbinado sugar

⭐ *If you're making your own rub and want to include sugar as an ingredient, it's best to use turbinado sugar, as it's less likely to burn inside the smoker.*

1 In a small sauté pan, toast the cumin seeds, coriander seeds, mustard seeds, and black peppercorns over medium heat for 1 to 2 minutes, or until fragrant. Let the spices cool and then grind them thoroughly in a spice grinder. Transfer the grind to a small bowl.

2 Add the salt, sweet paprika, and sugar. Mix thoroughly to combine well. Keep the rub in an airtight container.

SANTA MARIA RUB

★ **PREP TIME: 1 MINUTE** ★

Style: **CALIFORNIA**

MAKES ABOUT 1¼ CUPS   Here's a recipe from Michael Ollier, corporate chef for the Certified Angus Beef brand. Ollier says this is a "great go-to rub, created in honor of the classic grilled tri-tip made famous in California."

½ cup kosher salt
½ cup freshly ground black pepper
¼ cup granulated honey or turbinado sugar
1 tablespoon granulated garlic
1 tablespoon onion powder

1 In a small bowl, stir together the salt, pepper, granulated honey, garlic, and onion powder.

2 Store the rub in an airtight container in a cool, dark place.

⭐ *Granulated honey is a crystallized form of honey that is more convenient to use than regular honey but has the same great flavor. If you can't find it in the baking aisle of your supermarket, use turbinado sugar instead.*

RYAN LAMON

Ryan Lamon is the owner of Poppy + Rose, and Peaches' Smokehouse, a barbecue food truck in Los Angeles. Learn more at www.peachestruck.com.

Tell us your story.

I grew up in North Georgia. My dad had a barbecue restaurant called Frank's Real Pit BBQ in Hoschton. I worked with him a lot and got to a point where I was frustrated doing barbecue. So I ended up doing other things: Southeast Asian cuisine, French-Mediterranean bistros.

At the end of the day, I just wanted to barbecue again. When my wife Diana and I got out to LA, there was a noticeable lack of legitimate barbecue, and we decided that was the avenue we wanted to go.

How would you characterize Georgia barbecue?

It cherry-picks what it considers the best out of various barbecue cultures. When I was a kid, it was almost entirely pork butt. And it had a lot of western North Carolina influence: tomato-based sauces, lots of vinegar, heavy on the smoke.

But I think what really sets it apart is Brunswick stew as a side. In Georgia, depending on the region, it's vastly different.

What is your signature barbecue style?

I stay true to Georgian, Carolinian roots to a point. I think my time in other kitchens has altered that. Large chunks of meat, I always brine first. My brisket, for instance, is a marriage of Texas brisket and New York pastrami. It's brined for a significant period of time, then encrusted in peppercorn and brown sugar.

What are your thoughts on the future of barbecue?

What we're seeing is a lot of kids drawn to it because it's cool. The benefit is that you're getting young blood into it. The downside is you're going to see less of the regionally specific styles. It's going to become more of a melting pot.

 My brisket, for instance, is a marriage of Texas brisket and New York pastrami.

RYAN LAMON'S BRUNSWICK STEW

PREP TIME: 20 MINUTES ★ COOK TIME: 1½ HOURS

Style: GEORGIA

SERVES 10 TO 12   This recipe was handed down from Ryan Lamon's father, who owned a traditional pit barbecue joint in Hoschton, Georgia, called Frank's Real Pit BBQ. Brunswick stew is a typical side served with barbecue in Georgia; throughout the state it has regional variations. This version is the one that Lamon grew up eating, and it has chicken, pork, and beef in a tomato-based broth with corn and lima beans.

½ cup (1 stick) unsalted butter

2 onions, diced

5 garlic cloves, sliced

2 tablespoons freshly ground black pepper

2 tablespoons kosher salt, divided

2 pounds ground beef

4 cups low-sodium chicken broth

9 tomatoes, cored and pulsed in a
   food processor

2 tablespoons Worcestershire sauce

5 ears fresh corn, kernels removed from cob

4 cups lima beans, blanched

1 pound smoked and pulled pork shoulder

1 pound smoked and pulled chicken breast

⅔ cup distilled white vinegar

⅔ cup brown sugar

★ *When melting butter, wait until the foam subsides before adding ingredients to the pot.*

1 In a 5-quart pot, melt the butter over medium-high heat. Add the onions, garlic, black pepper, and ½ tablespoon of salt. Sauté the onions and garlic for 6 to 7 minutes, or until slightly softened.

2 Add the ground beef and season it with ½ tablespoon of salt. Cook the meat until it is browned.

3 Add the chicken broth, tomatoes, and Worcestershire sauce and cook them for 5 minutes. Add the corn, lima beans, pork, and chicken, reduce the heat to low, and simmer the stew for 30 minutes to 1 hour.

4 Add the vinegar, brown sugar, and remaining 1 tablespoon of salt. Cook for 5 to 10 more minutes. Serve immediately

BLACK BARBECUE SAUCE

★ PREP TIME: 5 MINUTES ★
COOK TIME: 10 MINUTES, PLUS OVERNIGHT TO CHILL

Style: WESTERN KENTUCKY

MAKES ABOUT 2 CUPS This Worcestershire-based sauce (more like a thin dip, really) is the must-have accompaniment for lamb. Allspice is key to helping tame the gamey flavor of the meat.

1 cup Worcestershire sauce

½ cup distilled white vinegar

½ cup water

Juice of 1 lemon

1 teaspoon ground allspice

1 tablespoon brown sugar

1 In a small pot, combine the Worcestershire sauce, vinegar, water, lemon juice, allspice, and sugar. Bring it to a simmer and cook for 5 to 10 minutes, or until the mixture is slightly thickened and the sugar has dissolved.

2 Let the sauce cool and then refrigerate it overnight before using.

⭐ *If you like your sauce a little bit thicker and with a bit of tomato flavor, some restaurants are known to use a bit of tomato paste. Stir in 1 tablespoon with the rest of the ingredients, and adjust from there to taste.*

MISSISSIPPI-STYLE BARBECUE SAUCE

★ PREP TIME: 5 MINUTES ★
COOK TIME: 5 MINUTES, PLUS OVERNIGHT TO CHILL

Style: MISSISSIPPI

MAKES ABOUT ⅔ CUP The Mississippi style is all about sweet, thick, red sauces.

1 tablespoon unsalted butter
1 tablespoon tomato paste
¼ cup apple cider vinegar
½ cup ketchup
½ cup brown sugar
1 teaspoon sweet paprika
1 teaspoon kosher salt
1 teaspoon cayenne pepper

⭐ *Tomato paste functions as a thickener and a concentrated source of tomato flavor.*

1 In a small pot, melt the butter over medium heat. Add the tomato paste and cook it for 1 minute, or until fragrant. Add the vinegar, ketchup, sugar, paprika, salt, and cayenne. Bring the sauce to a simmer and cook for 2 to 3 minutes, or until it's nice and thick and the sugar has dissolved.

2 Let the sauce cool and refrigerate it overnight before using.

JOHN RIVERS

John Rivers is the owner of 4 Rivers Smokehouse in Florida, where he specializes in Texas-style brisket. Every year, Rivers participates in the South Beach Food & Wine Festival and twice has been invited to cook at the James Beard House in New York City. Learn more at www.4rsmokehouse.com.

What are your thoughts on wrapping?

I did it for many years. There's a point during the cooking process where brisket simply won't absorb any more smoke, and from there you're really just baking it. Wrapping it protects the meat from drying out and expedites the smoking process. But, you lose that crunch on the bark and caramel color, because the sugars and proteins don't caramelize.

How important is it to trim brisket before cooking?

There are two schools of thought: Trim before cooking and then just slice and serve afterward, or leave all the fat on and trim the big pockets off after cooking, as you're slicing. I don't trim my brisket before cooking it. If there are big chunks of white, hard fat, I'll take that out, but otherwise all that fat is a great natural moisturizer.

Any other advice?

Always cook fat-side up, or all that fat's just gonna drip.

And when you pull brisket out of the smoker, immediately wrap it in plastic, put it in a cooler, and let it rest. I wrap in plastic versus aluminum foil because foil is going to leak, which is counterproductive to maintaining all the juice inside. Throw a towel over the wrapped brisket, press down on it, and keep it in the cooler for six to eight hours.

How would you define Floridian barbecue?

From a flavor perspective, it still is pork down here, but people are discovering brisket and jumping on that.

From a sauce perspective, you've got such diversity. Northeast Florida: mustard sauce. Central Florida: tomato based. And down south, you have a lot of Cuban influence.

 Always cook fat-side up, or all that fat's just gonna drip.

JOHN RIVERS'S SMOKED BRISKET

★ PREP TIME: 5 HOURS, PLUS OVERNIGHT TO CHILL ★
COOK TIME: 12 TO 18 HOURS, PLUS 1 TO 2 HOURS TO REST

Style: FLORIDA

SERVES 20   "Nothing will have as much impact on your brisket as the proper control and monitoring of the internal and external temperatures. Don't be discouraged by your first attempts. Smoking a good brisket is well worth the time and effort. And I'm willing to bet that, unlike me, it won't take you 18 years." —*John Rivers*

½ cup freshly ground black pepper
4 teaspoons kosher salt
4 teaspoons sugar
4 teaspoons onion powder
4 teaspoons garlic powder
4 teaspoons dried parsley
4 teaspoons dried oregano
4 teaspoons chili powder
1 (10- to 15-pound) whole packer brisket, untrimmed with full fat cap
Vegetable oil, for brushing the grates

⭐ *Depending on the size of your brisket, smoking will take from 12 to 18 hours. A general rule of thumb is 75 minutes for every pound of brisket.*

LEVEL OF DIFFICULTY
ADVANCED

RECOMMENDED WOOD
HICKORY

1 In a small bowl, mix together the pepper, salt, sugar, onion powder, garlic powder, dried parsley, dried oregano, and chili powder.

2 Thoroughly coat the brisket with the rub and refrigerate it, uncovered, for at least 4 hours, or preferably overnight.

3 One hour before smoking, remove the brisket from the refrigerator and let it stand at room temperature.

4 Preheat the smoker to 200°F to 225°F.

5 If using wood chips or chunks, soak them in water for at least 15 to 30 minutes. Add them to the smoker following the manufacturer's instructions.

6 Oil the smoker grates and place the brisket on them, fat-side up. Close the cooking compartment and cook the brisket for 8 to 10 hours. Add wood and fuel as necessary to maintain the smoke and temperature in the smoker.

➺

➤ JOHN RIVERS'S SMOKED BRISKET

7 Check the internal temperature using a meat thermometer inserted into the thickest part of the brisket. Continue cooking the meat until the internal temperature reaches 190°F to 192°F.

8 Remove the brisket from the smoker. Wrap it in multiple layers of plastic wrap and place it in a small cooler. Cover the brisket with a folded towel, close the cooler lid, and let the meat rest for 1 to 2 hours before carving.

9 When ready to serve, remove the brisket from the cooler and place it on a rimmed baking sheet. Cut open the plastic wrap, allowing the juices to spill out into the pan.

10 Transfer the brisket to a cutting board and, starting at the thinnest part of the flat, slice the brisket against the grain, working toward the thicker side (the point). Trim off the fat cap to your preference.

11 As you work your way up the brisket, you'll begin to notice a seam of fat forming in the middle of the brisket. This is the connective tissue that holds the flat and the point together. Once it becomes distinct and runs the entire width of the brisket, you need to separate the two cuts. Using a long knife and cutting the full width of the brisket, slice directly into the seam of fat along the contours of the meat until the two pieces are separated.

12 Remove the point, flip it over, and use the back of your knife to scrape the excess fat from the meat. Repeat on the bottom piece. Rotate the point 90 degrees so the grains of both pieces are running in the same direction. Flip both pieces over so the bark is facing up and continue carving as needed.

FULL MOON BAR-B-QUE'S HALF-MOON COOKIES

PREP TIME: 20 MINUTES ★ COOK TIME: 8 MINUTES

Style: ALABAMA

MAKES ABOUT 4 DOZEN These cookies are incredibly addictive, and it's awfully hard to eat just one. They have the perfect balance of sweetness and chocolaty flavor.

2¼ cups all-purpose flour

1 teaspoon baking soda

1 teaspoon salt

1 cup (2 sticks) unsalted butter, at room temperature

¾ cup granulated sugar

¾ cup light brown sugar, packed

2 large eggs

1 teaspoon pure vanilla extract

3 cups semi-sweet chocolate chips

1 cup pecans, chopped

1 (1-pound) Hershey chocolate bar

⭐ *Using a double boiler to melt chocolate prevents it from scorching.*

1 Preheat the oven to 375°F.

2 In a medium bowl, sift together the flour, baking soda, and salt. Set it aside.

3 In the bowl of an electric mixer, cream the butter, granulated sugar, and brown sugar on medium speed for 3 minutes. With the mixer running, add the eggs and vanilla. Mix until the eggs are fully incorporated.

4 On low speed, add the flour mixture, scraping down the sides, until fully incorporated. Turn off the mixer and stir in the chocolate chips and pecans.

5 Use a rounded teaspoon to scoop out the dough, 2 inches apart, onto an ungreased baking sheet.

6 Bake the cookies for 8 to 10 minutes. Let them cool for 1 minute, then transfer the cookies to a wire rack to cool completely. Refrigerate the cookies until completely cold.

7 Bring 1 inch of water to a simmer in a medium pot, and place a heat-proof bowl snugly over the top of the pot.

8 Add the chocolate to the bowl and melt it, stirring occasionally with a spatula.

9 Dip half of each refrigerated cookie into the melted chocolate. Set them on a sheet pan to cool.

MODERN INFLUENCES

fter a thorough examination of existing barbecue traditions, it's only natural to wonder: What's next? No cuisine, after all, is static. Rather, outside influences help it evolve over time, and barbecue is no exception. After all, barbecue in this country began as a way for Native Americans to cook game over a spit; over time, British, African American, German, Czech, and Greek traditions helped define the regional styles barbecue enthusiasts know and love today. In this chapter, another pitmaster gazes into the looking glass and offers his take on the future of barbecue: Johneric Concordia, a Filipino American pitmaster whose Los Angeles restaurant marries Filipino flavors with American-style cuts of meat.

make them your own. It's a two-way street, in other words. Marinades, rubs, sauces, and different ways of serving barbecue can all be combined to create a signature style.

PROTEINS

When it comes to getting creative with proteins, there are two approaches you can take. One is to think of new ways of cooking traditional cuts like pork shoulders, brisket, ribs, and sausage. Another is to think of new cuts or types of meat altogether. Anything that has plenty of fat (and ideally collagen, too) to render out during a low-and-slow cooking process is definitely worth trying.

Johneric Concordia has a particularly interesting example of the first approach. "You've got Kansas City champions who are making smoked sausages in a tamale wrapper so you don't have to use intestines as the sausage wrappers. It's an open-faced sausage, really, with no husk, and they're just utilizing the texture of the tamale. The graininess, those extra ridges, create surface area that holds the smoke."

FLAVORS, RUBS, AND SAUCES

There are plenty of ways to get creative here, but there's no need to reinvent the wheel. Start with the dishes from your favorite cuisines and think of ways to either incorporate their flavors into traditional barbecue, or to use traditional barbecue to

FILL THE PLATE

The concept of the "meat and three veg" meal disappeared long ago in most American dining establishments, but in barbecue it still persists in the form of barbecue trays and barbecue plates. And there will always be a place for that, just as there will always be a place for the venerable barbecue sandwich.

But, outside the realm of barbecue, home cooks and diners are increasingly shifting away from having meat at the center of the plate. Instead, they are using it sparingly as a flavoring element in vegetable-centric dishes. There are many reasons behind this, chief among them health and environmental concerns, but the rising cost of meat is certainly a key factor, too. So what does this mean for barbecue?

Well, one possibility is a blurring of the line between main dishes and side dishes. In a way, this trend has already begun, although it is certainly in its infancy. Memphis has always been fairly creative in coming up with these types of dishes, and barbecue stew is a great example. At its heart is perfectly smoked pulled pork, but there's a lot of other stuff going on (read: vegetables) that makes it a well-balanced meal—corn, okra, tomatoes, and beans. In Alabama, barbecue salads are some of the most popular lunch items. And in New York, admittedly about as far from the South as you can get, a popular burrito joint works smoked brisket into a rice bowl with pickled red onion, Cotija cheese, and habanero salsa.

POPULAR PAIRINGS

In the other chapters, this section has been dedicated to some fairly specific recommendations for drink pairings. But this chapter is all about thinking outside the box, so here is some general advice.

Whatever flavors you choose to incorporate into your barbecue should have some bearing on the beverage choice, but there's a lot of room for creativity. In general, you can take one of two approaches: complement the flavors in your barbecue, or contrast them. One thing probably worth remembering is that because your dish will always have some smoky flavor going on, anything that's overly bitter (like super hoppy IPAs or very tannic wines) won't work well. Beverages with smoky flavors—like mescal or smoked porters—tend to be polarizing: People either think the extra smoke flavor is great, or it just ends up being overwhelming.

POINTS TO REMEMBER

★ **Start small.** Focus on one cuisine, and stock your pantry.

★ **Seek out new experiences.** Explore new neighborhoods in your city and seek out specialty grocery stores. Try new dishes when you travel.

★ **Find a good butcher.** A good butcher can recommend new cuts and types of meat to smoke.

★ **Cook with a friend.** Everyone accumulates different food experiences, and cooking with a friend can be a source of inspiration.

★ **Take notes.** Being methodical can help you remember what worked and simplify the creative process.

PORK LOIN AL PASTOR

★ PREP TIME: 30 MINUTES, PLUS OVERNIGHT TO BRINE ★
COOK TIME: 3½ TO 4 HOURS, PLUS 1 HOUR TO REST

Style: MEXICAN

SERVES 18 TO 20   Pork loin is not a traditional cut for barbecue because it is very lean. However, if marinated overnight, it remains juicy and flavorful during the smoking process, and it's quick-cooking for its size.

1 (7- to 8-pound) whole boneless pork loin
8 cups Pineapple-Garlic Marinade (page 242)
1 cup Chili Dry Rub (page 241)
Vegetable oil, for brushing the grates

⭐ *Because the loin is such a large, uniform cut, it offers the perfect opportunity to experiment. Try rubbing different portions of the loin with different dry rubs.*

LEVEL OF DIFFICULTY
BEGINNER

RECOMMENDED WOOD
APPLE OR CHERRY

1 In a nonreactive container, submerge the pork loin in the Pineapple-Garlic Marinade and refrigerate it overnight.

2 Remove the loin from the marinade and pat it dry. Discard the marinade. Coat the loin thoroughly with the Chili Dry Rub and let it stand for 1 hour.

3 Preheat the smoker to 200°F to 225°F.

4 If using wood chips or chunks, soak them in water for at least 15 to 30 minutes. Add them to the smoker following the manufacturer's instructions.

5 Oil the smoker grates and place the pork loin on them. Close the cooking compartment and smoke the meat for 3½ to 4 hours, or until an instant-read thermometer reads 140°F. Add wood and fuel as necessary to maintain the smoke and temperature in the smoker.

6 Remove the pork loin from the smoker and let it rest for 1 hour. Slice and chop the pork into bite-size pieces to serve.

KICKED-UP
CHICKEN TORTILLA SOUP

PREP TIME: 15 MINUTES ★ **COOK TIME: 25 MINUTES**

Style: TEX-MEX

SERVES 4   This is no ordinary chicken tortilla soup. When you're starting with barbecued chicken cooked low and slow, there's no way it can be ordinary. Customize each bowl with your favorite toppings—avocado, chopped cilantro, Cotija cheese (also known as queso fresco), or lime juice—for the perfect balance of flavors in every bite.

1 tablespoon ground cumin

2 teaspoons onion powder

1 teaspoon garlic powder

Kosher salt to taste

1 teaspoon ground ancho chile

1 teaspoon ground chipotle chile

1 teaspoon ground guajillo chile

6 cups low-sodium chicken broth

1 (14-ounce) can tomato sauce

1 smoked chicken carcass (optional)

1 smoked chicken breast, meat pulled off the bone and chopped

1 smoked chicken leg (thigh plus drumstick), meat pulled off the bone and chopped

2 smoked chicken wings, meat pulled off the bone

3 corn tortillas, cut into strips

1 avocado, cubed (optional)

1 cup crumbled Cotija cheese

¼ cup chopped fresh cilantro

1 In a large pot, combine the cumin, onion powder, garlic powder, kosher salt to taste, ancho chile, chipotle chile, guajillo chile, chicken broth, tomato sauce, and chicken carcass (if using).

2 Bring the liquid to a simmer and cook the soup for 15 to 20 minutes to allow the flavors to blend. Remove the chicken carcass (if using).

3 Add the breast meat, leg meat, and wing meat and simmer for 3 to 4 minutes to allow the flavors to meld.

4 Add the tortilla strips to the soup and simmer for about 1 minute, or until softened.

5 Top with the avocado, cilantro, and Cotija cheese—or other optional toppings.

6 Serve immediately.

⭐ *Feel free to simmer the soup a bit longer if you'd like a thicker consistency.*

TACOS AL PASTOR

Style: MEXICAN

SERVES 4   Traditionally, the meat for these tacos is carved off a rotating spit and served in warm corn tortillas with a topping of fresh pineapple. It's simply street food at its best.

4 cups chopped pork from Pork Loin al Pastor (page 235)

12 (5-inch) corn tortillas, warmed

1½ cups Salsa Verde (page 243)

1½ cups finely chopped fresh pineapple

¾ cup finely chopped red or white onion

12 fresh cilantro sprigs

Divide the pork among the tortillas. Top each with about 2 tablespoons of Salsa Verde, 2 tablespoons of pineapple, 1 tablespoon of onion, and 1 cilantro sprig.

⭐ *To warm tortillas in the microwave, place a stack between two damp paper towels and microwave on high for 10 to 15 seconds.*

ZA'ATAR-SPICED LEG OF LAMB

★ **PREP TIME: 1 HOUR** ★

COOK TIME: 7½ TO 9 HOURS, PLUS 1 HOUR TO REST

Style: **EASTERN MEDITERRANEAN**

SERVES 12   Za'atar is a spice blend with Eastern Mediterranean origins, a heady mixture of thyme, sesame seeds, and sumac, a citrusy dried spice that comes from a shrub native to the region.

2 tablespoons sesame seeds

2 tablespoons dried thyme

2 tablespoons sumac

6 tablespoons kosher salt

1 (5- to 6-pound) bone-in leg of lamb

Vegetable oil, for brushing the grates

⭐ *You can find sumac in specialty Indian and Middle Eastern groceries, or online through retailers like Kalustyan's (www.kalustyans.com) and Patel Brothers (www.patelbros.com).*

LEVEL OF DIFFICULTY
INTERMEDIATE

RECOMMENDED WOOD
HICKORY

1 To make the za'atar, in a small sauté pan, toast the sesame seeds, thyme, and sumac over medium heat for 1 to 2 minutes, or until fragrant. Let the spices cool, then grind them thoroughly in a spice grinder. Transfer the grind to a small bowl.

2 Add the salt and mix thoroughly. Store in an airtight container.

3 Trim the fat from the lamb, and season it with the za'atar (see page 44). Let it stand at room temperature for 1 hour.

4 Preheat the smoker to 225°F to 275°F.

5 If using wood chips or chunks, soak them in water for at least 15 to 30 minutes. Add them to the smoker following the manufacturer's instructions.

6 Oil the smoker grates and place the lamb on them, fat-side up. Close the cooking compartment and smoke the meat for 7½ to 9 hours, or until an instant-read thermometer inserted without touching the bone reads 190°F. Add wood and fuel as necessary to maintain the smoke and temperature in the smoker.

7 Remove the lamb from the smoker and let it rest for 1 hour. Discard the bones and chop the meat into bite-sized pieces.

LAMB GYROS WITH YOGURT-DILL SAUCE

★ **PREP TIME: 15 MINUTES** ★

Style: MEDITERRANEAN

SERVES 4   The yogurt-dill sauce, which gets a nice zip from minced garlic, stands in cool contrast to the rich, smoky lamb in these delectable lamb gyros.

4 cups chopped lamb from Za'atar-Spiced
  Leg of Lamb (page 239)
12 small pitas, toasted
1½ cups Yogurt-Dill Sauce (page 244)
¾ cup finely diced tomatoes
¾ cup finely diced cucumber
¾ cup finely diced red onion

⭐ *To toast the pita bread, slather the outsides with about 1 tablespoon of olive oil and place on a warm griddle or grill for 3 to 4 minutes per side.*

Divide the lamb among the 12 pitas. Top each with about 2 tablespoons of Yogurt-Dill Sauce and 1 tablespoon each of the tomatoes, cucumber, and onion.

CHILI DRY RUB

PREP TIME: 3 MINUTES ★ **COOK TIME: 2 MINUTES**

Style: MEXICAN

MAKES ABOUT ⅓ CUP Ground guajillo chiles give this dry rub a distinctive, fruity heat.

1 teaspoon black peppercorns
1 teaspoon whole cloves
2 teaspoons cumin seeds
2 tablespoons ground guajillo chile
2 teaspoons kosher salt
1 teaspoon cayenne pepper
1 teaspoon turbinado sugar

⭐ *This spice rub will store in a cool, dark place for up to 1 year.*

1 In a small sauté pan, toast the black peppercorns, cloves, and cumin seeds over medium heat for 1 to 2 minutes, or until fragrant. Let them cool and then grind them thoroughly in a spice grinder. Transfer the grind to a small bowl.

2 Add the ground guajillo chile, salt, cayenne, and sugar. Mix thoroughly to combine the ingredients. Keep in an airtight container.

PINEAPPLE-GARLIC MARINADE

PREP TIME: 1 MINUTE ★ **COOK TIME: 10 MINUTES**

Style: MEXICAN

MAKES ABOUT 2 CUPS   This pineapple-garlic marinade is ideal for lean cuts of meat like pork loin and chicken.

1 cup extra-virgin olive oil
10 garlic cloves, smashed
1 tablespoon dried oregano
½ cup pineapple juice
Juice of ½ lime
Juice of 1½ oranges
1 tablespoon kosher salt
1 bunch cilantro, stems only

⭐ *Marinades should always contain an acid, an oil, salt, sugar, and flavoring agents such as onions, garlic, chiles, and herbs.*

1 In a small pot, heat the oil, garlic, and oregano over medium heat for 1 to 2 minutes, or until fragrant.

2 Turn off the heat, let the oil cool to room temperature, then add the pineapple juice, lime juice, orange juice, salt, and cilantro stems.

3 Transfer the marinade to an airtight container and refrigerate it until completely chilled before using.

SALSA VERDE

★ **PREP TIME: 5 MINUTES** ★

Style: MEXICAN

MAKES ABOUT 1 CUP This fresh, tangy sauce made with tomatillos is fantastic with chicken, beef, or pork. For an interesting twist, try roasting the tomatillos first.

¼ cup extra-virgin olive oil

4 ounces tomatillos, cored and coarsely chopped

2 cups fresh flat-leaf parsley leaves

1 cup fresh cilantro leaves

1 jalapeño, seeded and coarsely chopped

1 teaspoon kosher salt

1 teaspoon red pepper flakes

Juice of ½ lime

1 In the bowl of a small food processor, combine the olive oil, tomatillos, parsley, cilantro, jalapeño, salt, red pepper flakes, and lime juice. Process thoroughly.

2 Use the salsa immediately or transfer to an airtight container and refrigerate.

⭐ *This salsa will stay fresh in the refrigerator for up to 5 days.*

YOGURT-DILL SAUCE

★ PREP TIME: 5 MINUTES ★

Style: EASTERN MEDITERRANEAN

SERVES 6 Fans of creamy dressings often have trouble switching to lighter vinaigrettes. Some resort to using low-fat, store-bought mayonnaise, which often has more sugar and salt than its full-fat counterparts (the loss of flavor has to be compensated for somehow). Here's a better solution: nonfat Greek yogurt. It transforms classic lemon vinaigrette into a creamy, yet light dressing that's fit for sturdier greens like kale, and hearty salad classics like potato salad.

6 tablespoons extra-virgin olive oil
2 tablespoons freshly squeezed lemon juice
¾ cup nonfat Greek yogurt
¼ cup chopped fresh dill
5 garlic cloves, minced
Kosher salt
Freshly ground black pepper

1 In a medium bowl, slowly whisk the olive oil and lemon juice until they are emulsified, then whisk in the Greek yogurt.

2 Stir in the chopped dill, followed by the garlic; season the sauce with salt and pepper.

⭐ *When buying dill, the fronds should be deep green and look lively; avoid bunches with yellowing or browning tips.*

JOHNERIC CONCORDIA

Johneric Concordia is the co-owner, co-founder, and BBQist of the Park's Finest in Los Angeles, a restaurant that smokes American barbecue cuts with Filipino flavor. Learn more about their food at www.theparksfinest.com.

Tell me a bit about your background with barbecue.

My father emigrated here from the Philippines through the Navy. He would have cookouts on the destroyer, and when he came here, he continued the same tradition of using whatever was in the kitchen. So he was always asked to barbecue at house parties. Growing up, I was the kid standing next to dad, helping keep an eye on the meat.

How would you describe your signature barbecue style?

We call it the Los Angeles approach, utilizing indirect smoke and pellet technology to get food to a particular texture and temperature, with Filipino flavors: pepper, garlic, onion dry rub, and sauce on the side. The sauce, or *sawsawan*, is a variation of what my dad made over the years for gatherings.

What is your best-known dish?

My mother's coconut beef is a stew that comes from my grandmother's region of Real, Quezon. The area is known throughout the archipelago for the people's creative uses of coconut and fresh seafood. Traditionally, they would boil water buffalo for days—it's a tough meat—and then let it stew with garlic, coconut cream, fish sauce, and chiles. What we do here at the Park's Finest is smoke top round for 16 hours, cube it, stew it in a coconut gravy, and then put it back into the smoker to absorb more smoke. The coconut beef is served over a bed of fluffy white jasmine rice.

What are your thoughts on the future of barbecue?

I think as technology advances, the methods and understanding of barbecue will continue to advance as well. There are going to be more hobbyists; folks are going to get into it. People all over the world have employed different methods of grilling, smoking, and barbecuing. As we continue to be exposed to more styles and flavor profiles, the creativity and accessibility for people to create great barbecue will continue to flourish.

 I think as technology advances, the methods and understanding of barbecue will continue to advance as well.

JOHNERIC CONCORDIA'S SMOKED BEEF MARROW AND BULALO SOUP

★ **PREP TIME: 1 HOUR** ★ **COOK TIME: 2 DAYS**

Style: LOS ANGELES–FILIPINO

SERVES 15 "In the Philippine archipelago's northern island of Luzon, the provincial region of Batangas is known for its coconuts, cattle, butterfly knives, and beef bone marrow soup. Here's my rendition of *batangueño bulalo* (beef soup) with an L.A. accent. This is a soup that demands dedication, determination, and a deep pot." —*Johneric Concordia*

FOR THE PEPPER BLEND

1 cup freshly ground white pepper

1 cup freshly ground black pepper

½ cup plus 2 tablespoons red pepper flakes

3½ tablespoons chili powder

FOR THE SAVORY BLEND

1¾ cups garlic powder

1¾ cups granulated garlic

1½ cups minced garlic

2½ cups onion powder

2½ cups granulated onion

1¾ CUPS CHOPPED ONION FOR THE BEEF BROTH

15 pounds beef joint knuckles, neck bones, and/or split femurs

¾ cup extra-virgin olive oil

3¾ tablespoons pink Himalayan salt

Pepper Blend

Savory Blend

2 cups sugar cane vinegar

⅜ cup fish sauce, preferably Three Crabs brand

1 cup dry red wine

FOR THE SMOKED BONE MARROW

6 (6-inch) center-cut split beef femurs (about 10 pounds)

¾ cup extra-virgin olive oil

1¼ tablespoons pink Himalayan salt

½ cup Pepper Blend

Savory Blend

Vegetable oil, for brushing the grates

Green shallots, thinly sliced, for garnish

Jasmine rice, cooked, for serving

Lemon wedges, for serving

Salt, for serving

Freshly ground black pepper, for serving

Vinegar, for serving

Fish sauce, for serving

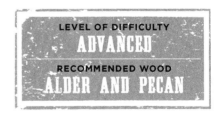

LEVEL OF DIFFICULTY
ADVANCED

RECOMMENDED WOOD
ALDER AND PECAN

➤➤ JOHNERIC CONCORDIA'S SMOKED BEEF MARROW AND BULALO SOUP

⭐ *Green shallots are a regional farmers' market treat that appear in the spring. If you can't find green shallots, green onions or spring onions are a good substitute. Feel free to play with the measurements of some of the ingredients, too; this version of the soup was converted and scaled down from a recipe used in restaurants.*

TO MAKE THE PEPPER BLEND

In a medium bowl, mix together the white pepper, black pepper, red pepper flakes, and chili powder. Set aside.

TO MAKE THE SAVORY BLEND

In another medium bowl, mix together the garlic powder, granulated garlic, minced garlic, onion powder, granulated onion, and chopped onion. Set aside.

TO MAKE THE BEEF BROTH

1 Preheat the oven to 375°F.

2 Place the beef bones in a large roasting pan (you may need to do this in batches). Drizzle the bones with the olive oil, then season them in this order: pink salt, Pepper Blend to taste, and Savory Blend to taste. Roast the bones for 45 minutes. Then turn the bones over and roast them for 45 minutes more.

3 Transfer the roasted bones to a 20-quart pot and submerge them in cool water. Add the vinegar and fish sauce. Let the bones rest for 30 minutes.

4 Deglaze the roasting pan with the red wine and add the contents to the pot.

5 Bring the liquid in the pot to a boil; skim off any foam and excess fat that comes to the surface. Reduce the heat to a slow simmer. Every 8 hours, skim off the fat and add more water to keep the bones submerged. After 24 hours, strain the broth into another pot. Separate the tendons, marrow, and meat from the bones and refrigerate them until completely cold.

6 Return the bones to the pot with the broth and add enough water to submerge the bones. Bring the broth to a boil. then reduce the heat to a slow simmer and continue to simmer the broth for another 24 hours. Skim any remaining fat from the broth. The broth will turn mahogany in color.

7 Remove the bones from the broth and cool the broth completely.

TO MAKE THE SMOKED BONE MARROW

1 Drizzle the femur bones with the olive oil, then season them in this order: pink salt, Pepper Blend, and a generous amount of the Savory Blend.

2 Preheat the smoker to 160°F.

3 If using wood chips or chunks, soak them in water for at least 15 to 30 minutes. Add them to the smoker following the manufacturer's instructions.

4 Oil the smoker grates and place the bones on them. Close the cooking compartment and smoke the bones for 10 hours. Add wood and fuel as necessary to maintain the smoke and temperature in the smoker.

5 To serve, place the reserved tendons, marrow, and meat in a large pot with the beef broth, and bring it to a boil. For each serving, ladle 2 cups of hot broth into a bowl, add ¼ cup of the tendon mixture, and garnish with 2 tablespoons of sliced green shallots. Serve with small bowls of rice and small saucers of lemon wedges, salt, pepper, vinegar, and fish sauce.

ACKNOWLEDGMENTS

First of all, I'd like to thank Clara Song Lee, my managing editor, for making this project possible. It has always been a pleasure working with you, and I am sure that this cookbook is only one of many more to come. And, of course, I'd be remiss in not giving my heartfelt thanks to all of the hardworking people at Callisto Media and the mighty team of freelancers who ensured that this book made it through every step of the production process on time (well, more or less, mea culpa for any deadlines I missed!).

Mike Barbera, thank you for giving me the time to work on this project. Your generosity will always be remembered.

I'd like to give a big shout out to everyone who contributed their interesting stories, know-how, and recipes to this book: William Weisiger, Ryan Lamon, Clint Cantwell, David and Joe Maluff, John Rivers, Doc and Susan Richardson, Michael Ollier, and Johneric Concordia. Special thanks to Lulu Phongmany for connecting me with your partners in meat worship, Tyson Ho and John Tesar. And thank you to Brailyn Hardy at KC Projects, Haley Finucane at Bread & Butter PR, Major at Rockaway PR, and Russell Powell at Lou Hammond & Associates for keeping the ball rolling. Kate Izor, thank you for finally making me look normal in a headshot. For that, you deserve your own paragraph.

I also would like to express my gratitude to my family for supporting me during the development of this book (thank you for eating all of the food) and letting me smoke things for hours on end (sorry about all the char marks on the ground).

Lastly, and most importantly, thank you to Deepak Venkatachalam, who had to put up with my absence during a New York winter, while I barbecued the hours away in Los Angeles. One of these days, I will write a book about vegetables, just for you.

MEASUREMENTS AND CONVERSIONS

VOLUME EQUIVALENTS (LIQUID)

US STANDARD	US STANDARD (OUNCES)	METRIC (APPROXIMATE)
2 tablespoons	1 fl. oz.	30 mL
¼ cup	2 fl. oz.	60 mL
½ cup	4 fl. oz.	120 mL
1 cup	8 fl. oz.	240 mL
1½ cups	12 fl. oz.	355 mL
2 cups or 1 pint	16 fl. oz.	475 mL
4 cups or 1 quart	32 fl. oz.	1 L
1 gallon	128 fl. oz.	4 L

VOLUME EQUIVALENTS (DRY)

US STANDARD	METRIC (APPROXIMATE)
⅛ teaspoon	0.5 mL
¼ teaspoon	1 mL
½ teaspoon	2 mL
¾ teaspoon	4 mL
1 teaspoon	5 mL
1 tablespoon	15 mL
¼ cup	59 mL
⅓ cup	79 mL
½ cup	118 mL
⅔ cup	156 mL
¾ cup	177 mL
1 cup	235 mL
2 cups or 1 pint	475 mL
3 cups	700 mL
4 cups or 1 quart	1 L
½ gallon	2 L
1 gallon	4 L

OVEN TEMPERATURES

FAHRENHEIT (F)	CELSIUS (C) (APPROXIMATE)
250°F	120°C
300°F	150°C
325°F	165°C
350°F	180°C
375°F	190°C
400°F	200°C
425°F	220°C
450°F	230°C

WEIGHT EQUIVALENTS

US STANDARD	METRIC (APPROXIMATE)
½ ounce	15 g
1 ounce	30 g
2 ounces	60 g
4 ounces	115 g
8 ounces	225 g
12 ounces	340 g
16 ounces or 1 pound	455 g

THE DIRTY DOZEN AND THE CLEAN FIFTEEN

A nonprofit and environmental watchdog organization called Environmental Working Group (EWG) looks at data supplied by the US Department of Agriculture (USDA) and the Food and Drug Administration (FDA) about pesticide residues and compiles a list each year of the best and worst pesticide loads found in commercial crops. You can refer to the Dirty Dozen list to know which fruits and vegetables you should always buy organic. The Clean Fifteen list lets you know which produce is considered safe enough when grown conventionally to allow you to skip the organics. This does not mean that the Clean Fifteen produce is pesticide-free, though, so wash these fruits and vegetables thoroughly. These lists change every year, so make sure you look up the most recent before you fill your shopping cart. You'll find the most recent lists as well as a guide to pesticides in produce at www.EWG.org/FoodNews.

2015	
DIRTY DOZEN	**CLEAN FIFTEEN**
Apples	Asparagus
Celery	Avocados
Cherry tomatoes	Cabbage
Cucumbers	Cantaloupe
Grapes	Cauliflower
Nectarines	Eggplant
Peaches	Grapefruit
Potatoes	Kiwis
Snap peas	Mangos
Spinach	Onions
Strawberries	Papayas
Sweet bell peppers	Pineapples
	Sweet corn
In addition to the Dirty Dozen, the EWG added two foods contaminated with highly toxic organo-phosphate insecticides:	Sweet peas (frozen)
	Sweet potatoes
Hot peppers	
Kale/Collard greens	

RESOURCES

MEAT, POULTRY, SEAFOOD, AND GAME

Bell & Evans
www.bellandevans.com

Copper River Salmon
www.copperriversalmon.org

D'Artagnan
www.heritagefoodsusa.com

Louisiana Crawfish Company
www.lacrawfish.com

Mary's Free-Range Chicken
www.maryschickens.com

Niman Ranch
www.nimanranch.com

Omaha Steaks
www.omahasteaks.com

SPICES AND SEASONINGS

Frank's RedHot
www.franksredhot.com

Kalustyan's
www.kalustyans.com

Morton & Bassett
www.mortonbassett.com

Old Bay
www.oldbay.com

Patel Brothers
www.patelbros.com

Tabasco
www.tabasco.com

BEER AND WHISKEY

Anchor Brewing
www.anchorbrewing.com

Blue Point Brewing Company
www.bluepointbrewing.com

Buffalo Trace Distillery
www.buffalotracedistillery.com

Bulleit Frontier Whiskey
www.bulleit.com

Chimay
www.chimay.com/en

Elijah Craig
www.heavenhill.com

Fat Tire
www.newbelgium.com

Goose Island Brewery
www.gooseisland.com

Köstritzer
www.bitburger-international.com

Lagunitas Brewing Company
www.lagunitas.com

Ommegang Brewery
www.ommegang.com

Paulaner
www.paulaner.com/en

Samuel Adams
www.samueladams.com

Spaten
www.spatenbeer.com

ONLINE BBQ INFORMATION

The BBQ Brethren
www.bbqbrethren.com

The BBQ Forum
www.bbqforum.com

The Smoke Ring
www.thesmokering.com

Grillocracy
www.grillocracy.com

The Texas BBQ Forum
www.texasbbqforum.com

BBQ COMPETITIONS

International Barbeque Cookers
Association
www.ibcabbq.org

Kansas City Barbeque Society
www.kcbs.us

Lonestar Barbecue Society
www.lonestarbarbecue.com

Memphis Barbecue Network
www.mbnbbq.com

New England Barbecue Society
www.nebs.org

North Carolina Barbecue Society
www.ncbbqsociety.com

St. Louis Barbecue Society
www.stlouisbbqsociety.com

BBQ PITMASTERS

Clint Cantwell
www.grillocracy.com

David and Joe Maluff
www.fullmoonbbq.com

Doc and Susan Richardson
www.docssmokehouse.com

John Rivers
www.4rsmokehouse.com

John Tesar
www.chefjohntesar.com

Johneric Concordia
www.theparksfinest.com

Michael Ollier
www.gorare.com/meatheads
/chef-michael

Ryan Lamon
www.peachestruck.com

Tyson Ho
www.arrogantswine.com

William Weisiger
www.ten50bbq.com

REFERENCES

Davis, Ardie A., Paul Kirk, and Carolyn Wells. *The Kansas City Barbecue Society Cookbook: 25th Anniversary Edition.* Kansas City: Andrews McMeel, 2010.

"The Evolution of Santa Maria BBQ." Santa Maria Valley: California's Barbecue Capital. Accessed January 19, 2016. santamariavalleybbq.com/2011/07/08/the-evolution-of-santa-maria-bbq.

Franklin, Aaron, and Jordan Mackay. *Franklin Barbecue: A Meat-Smoking Manifesto.* Berkeley: Ten Speed Press, 2015.

Freeman, Ashley S., *Southern Living Ultimate Book of BBQ.* New York: Oxmoor House, 2015.

Meek, Craig David. *Memphis Barbecue: A Succulent History of Smoke, Sauce & Soul.* Charleston, SC: The History Press, 2014.

Moss, Robert F. *Barbecue: The History of an American Institution.* Tuscaloosa: University of Alabama Press, 2010.

"The Origins of Santa Maria Tri-tip." Santa Maria Valley: California's Barbecue Capital. Accessed January 19, 2016. santamariavalleybbq.com/2009/12/17/the-origins-of-santa-maria-tri-tip.

Raichlen, Steven. "A Guide to Vertical Gas/Propane Smokers." Steven Raichlen's Barbecue! Bible. March 6, 2015. barbecuebible.com/2015/03/06/vertical-propane-gas-smokers.

Raichlen, Steven. "New Kid on the Block: Pellet Grills." Steven Raichlen's Barbecue! Bible. February 20, 2015. barbecuebible.com/2015/02/20/new-pellet-grills.

Reed, John Shelton, and Dale Volberg Reed. *Holy Smoke: The Big Book of North Carolina Barbecue.* Chapel Hill: University of North Carolina Press, 2008.

"Southern BBQ Trail." Southern Foodways Alliance. Accessed January 19, 2016. www.southernfoodways.org/oral-history/southern-bbq-trail.

Vaughn, Daniel. *The Prophets of Smoked Meat: A Journey through Texas Barbecue.* New York: HarperCollins, 2013.

Walsh, Robb. *Legends of Texas Barbecue Cookbook: Recipes and Recollections from the Pit Bosses.* San Francisco: Chronicle, 2002.

Ward, Edward. *The Barbacue Feast: Or the Three Pigs of Peckham.* London: B. Bragge, 1707.

RECIPE TYPE INDEX

SMOKING RECIPES BY LEVEL

SMOKING RECIPES BY PROTEIN

GENERAL BBQ RECIPES

INDEX

ABOUT THE AUTHOR

WILL BUDIAMAN is a New York City–based freelance writer and recipe developer. He is a graduate of the International Culinary Center and is the recipe editor for Blue Apron. Previously, he served as a recipe tester for Maple, worked as a web producer for *Bon Appétit* and Epicurious, and was a recipe editor at The Daily Meal, where he ran the test kitchen. Will has written four other cookbooks, including another book about barbecue, *Real BBQ: The Ultimate Step-by-Step Smoker Cookbook*. To learn more, visit willbudiaman.com.

CPSIA information can be obtained
at www.ICGtesting.com
Printed in the USA
LVOW06s0757241217
560581LV00008BA/9/P